.)]   ]]   2017

EYEWITNESS TRAVEL
PHRASE BOOK
GERMAN

D0829787

DK

REVISED EDITION

DK LONDON

Senior Editor Christine Stroyan
Senior Art Editors Anna Hall, Amy Child
Art Director Karen Self
Associate Publisher Liz Wheeler
Publishing Director Jonathan Metcalf
Proofreading Ingrid Price-Gschlossl, in association with
First Edition Translations Ltd, Cambridge, UK
Senior Pre-Producer Andy Hilliard
Senior Producers Gary Batchelor, Anna Vallarino

DK DELHI

Assistant Editor Sugandha Agarwal
Assistant Art Editor
Anukriti Arora
Art Editors Ravi Indiver, Mansi Agarwal
Senior Art Editor Chhaya Sajwan
Managing Editor Soma B. Chowdhury
Senior Managing Art Editor
Arunesh Talapatra

Production Manager Pankaj Sharma
Preproduction Managers
Sunil Sharma, Balwant Singh
Senior DTP Designers
Tarun Sharma, Vishal Bhatia,
Neeraj Bhatia, Ajay Verma

First American edition 2008
This revised edition published in 2017 by
DK Publishing,
345 Hudson Street, New York, New York 10014

A WORLD OF IDEAS:
SEE ALL THERE IS TO KNOW
www.dk.com

CONTENTS

INTRODUCTION

This book provides all the key words and phrases you are likely to need in everyday situations. It is grouped into themes, and key phrases are broken down into short sections to help you build a wide variety of sentences. A lot of the vocabulary is illustrated to make it easy to remember, and "You may hear" boxes feature questions you are likely to hear. At the back of the book there is a menu guide, listing about 500 food terms, and a 2,000-word two-way dictionary.

NOUNS

All German nouns (words for things, people, and ideas) are masculine, feminine, or neuter. The gender of singular nouns is shown by the word for "the": **der** (masculine), **die** (feminine), or **das** (neuter). **Die** is also used with plural nouns. You can look up the gender of words in the German–English dictionary at the back of the book. Some nouns, such as people's jobs or nationalities, change endings according to whether you are talking about a man or woman. In this book the masculine form is usually shown, followed by the feminine form:

I'm American	**Ich bin Amerikaner/Amerikanerin**
I'm Canadian	**Ich bin Kanadier/Kanadierin**

"A"

The word for "a" or "an" also changes according to gender. It is **ein** for masculine and neuter words and **eine** for feminine words. Alternatives are shown as below:

Another...please	**Noch ein/eine...bitte**

"YOU"

There are two ways of saying "you" when addressing someone in German: **Sie** (polite) and **du** (familiar). In this book we have used **Sie** throughout as this is what you normally use with people you don't know.

PRONUNCIATION GUIDE

Below each German word or phrase in this book, you will find a pronunciation guide. Read it as if it were English and you should be understood, but remember that it is only a guide and for the best results you should listen to the native speakers in the audio app and try to mimic them. Some German sounds are different from those in English, so take note of how the letters below are pronounced.

a	like "a" in "father"
ä	like "e" in "get"
au	like "ow" in "how"
äu, eu	like "oy" in "toy"
b	like "b" at the beginning of a word like "p" at the end of a word
ch	pronounced at the back of the throat, like "ch" in the Scottish word "loch"
d	like "d" in "dog" at the beginning of a word like "t" in "tin" at the end of a word
ei	like "y" in "by," or "i" in "pile"
i	like "i" in "hit," or "ee" in "see"
ie	like "ee" in "see"
j	like "y" in "yes"
ö	like "ur" in "burn"
qu	like "kv"
r	rolled at the back of the throat
s	like "s" in "see," "sh" in "ship," or "z" in "zoo"
sch	like "sh" in "shop"
ß	like "ss" in "grass"
u	like "oo" in "boot"

ü	like "ew" in "dew"
v	like "f" in "foot"
w	like "v" in "van"
z	like "ts" in "pets"

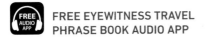

FREE EYEWITNESS TRAVEL PHRASE BOOK AUDIO APP

The audio app that accompanies this phrase book contains nearly 1,000 essential German words and phrases, spoken by native speakers, for use when traveling or when preparing for your trip.

HOW TO USE THE AUDIO APP

- Download the free app on your smartphone or tablet from the App Store or Google Play.
- Open the app and scan or key in the barcode on the back of your Eyewitness Phrase Book to add the book to your Library.
- Download the audio files for your language.
- The ⌂ symbol in the book indicates that there is audio for that section. Enter the page number from the book into the search field in the app to bring up the list of words and phrases for that page or section. You can then scroll up and down through the list to find the word or phrase you want.
- Tap a word or phrase to hear it.
- Swipe left or right to view the previous or next page.
- Add phrases you will use often to your Favorites.

ESSENTIALS

In this section, you will find the essential words and phrases you will need for basic everyday talk and situations. Be aware of cultural differences when you are addressing native German speakers, and remember that they tend to be rather formal when greeting each other. There are two ways of saying "you" in German. *Sie* is used for older people or people you don't know very well, whereas the more familiar *du* is used with family and friends.

GREETINGS

Hello

Guten Tag!
goo-ten tahk

Good evening

Guten Abend
goo-ten ah-bent

Good night

Gute Nacht
goo-te nakht

Goodbye

Auf Wiedersehen
owf vee-der-zay-en

Hi/bye!

Hi/Tschüss!
hi/tshews

Pleased to meet you

Sehr erfreut
zair air-froyt

How are you?

Wie geht es Ihnen?
vee gayt es ee-nen

Fine, thanks

Danke, gut
dun-ke goot

You're welcome

Nichts zu danken
nikhts tsoo dun-ken

My name is...

Ich heiße...
ikh hye-se

What's your name?

Wie heißen Sie?
vee hye-sen zee

What's his/her name?

Wie heißt er/sie?
vee hyst air/zee

This is...

Das ist...
dus ist

Nice to meet you

Freut mich
froyt mikh

See you tomorrow

Bis morgen
bis mor-gen

See you soon

Bis bald
bis bahlt

SMALL TALK 🎧

Yes/no	**Ja/Nein** *yah/nine*
Please	**Bitte** *bit-te*
Thank you (very much)	**Danke (vielen Dank)** *dun-ke (vee-len dunk)*
You're welcome	**Gern geschehen** *gairn ge-shay-en*
OK/fine	**OK/prima** *o-kay/pree-ma*
Pardon?	**Wie bitte?** *vee bit-te*
Excuse me	**Entschuldigung** *ent-shool-dee-gung*
Sorry	**Tut mir leid** *toot mir lite*
I don't know	**Ich weiß es nicht** *ikh vice es nikht*
I don't understand	**Ich verstehe Sie nicht** *ikh fair-shtay-ye zee nikht*
Could you repeat that?	**Könnten Sie das wiederholen?** *kurn-ten zee dus vee-der-ho-len*
I don't speak German	**Ich spreche nicht Deutsch** *ikh shpray-khe nikht doytsh*
Do you speak English?	**Sprechen Sie Englisch?** *shpray-ken zee eng-lish*
What is the German for...?	**Was heißt...auf Deutsch?** *vus hyst...owf doytsh*
What's that called?	**Wie heißt das?** *vee hyst dus*
Can you tell me...	**Können Sie mir sagen...** *kurnen zee mir zah-gen*

TALKING ABOUT YOURSELF

I'm from...	Ich komme aus... *ikh kom-me ows*
I'm...	Ich bin... *ikh bin*
...American	...Amerikaner/Amerikanerin *ah-meri-kah-ner/ah-meri-kah-ner-in*
...English	...Engländer/Engländerin *eng-len-der/eng-len-der-in*
...Canadian	...Kanadier/Kanadierin *kah-nah-dee-er/kah-nah-dee-er-in*
...Australian	...Australier/Australierin *ows-trah-lee-er/ows-trah-lee-er-in*
...single/married	...ledig/verheiratet *leh-dik/fair-hy-ra-tet*
...divorced	...geschieden *ge-shee-den*
I am...years old	Ich bin...Jahre alt *ikh bin...yah-re ult*
I have...	Ich habe... *ikh hah-be*
...a boyfriend	...einen Freund *ine-en froynt*
...a girlfriend	...eine Freundin *ine-e froyn-din*
...children	...kinder *kin-der*
Where are you from?	Wo kommen Sie her? *vo kom-men zee hair*
Are you married?	Sind Sie verheiratet? *zint zee fair-hy-ra-tet*
Do you have children?	Haben Sie Kinder? *hah-ben zee kin-der*

SOCIALIZING

Do you live here?	Wohnen Sie hier? *voh-nen zee heer*
Where do you live?	Wo wohnen Sie? *vo voh-nen zee*
I am here...	Ich bin hier... *ikh bin heer*
...on vacation	...im Urlaub *im oor-lowp*
...on business	...auf Dienstreise *owf deenst-rye-ze*
I'm a student	Ich bin Student/Studentin *ikh bin shtoo-dent/shtoo-den-tin*
I work in...	Ich arbeite in/im... *ikh ar-by-te in/im*
I am retired	Ich bin in Pension *ikh bin in pen-zee-on*
Can I...	Kann ich... *kunn ikh*
...have your telephone number?	...Ihre Telefonnummer haben? *ee-re tay-lay-fohn-noom-mer hah-ben*
...have your email address?	...Ihre E-Mail-Adresse haben? *ee-re e-mail-ah-dres-se hah-ben*
It doesn't matter	Das macht nichts *dus makht nikhts*
Cheers	Prost *prost*
I don't drink/smoke	Ich trinke/rauche nicht *ikh trin-ke/row-khe nikht*
Are you alright?	Wie geht es Ihnen? *vee gayt es ee-nen*
I'm OK	Es geht mir gut *es gayt mir goot*

LIKES AND DISLIKES

I like/love...	Ich mag/liebe... *ikh mahk/lee-be*
I don't like...	Ich mag keinen/keine/kein... *ikh mahk kine-en/kine-e/kine*
I hate...	Ich hasse... *ikh has-se*
I rather/really like...	Ich habe...ganz/sehr gern *ikh hah-be...gunts/zair gern*
Don't you like it?	Mögen Sie das nicht? *mur-gen zee dus nikht*
I would like...	Ich möchte gern... *ikh murkh-te gairn*
I'd like this one/that one	Ich möchte das hier/dort *ikh murkh-te dus heer/dort*
My favorite is...	Am liebsten mag ich... *um leep-sten mahk ikh*
I prefer...	Ich mag lieber... *ikh mahk lee-ber*
I think it's great/awful	Ich finde es toll/schrecklich *ikh fin-de es toll/shrek-likh*
What would you like to do?	Was möchten Sie gern tun? *vus murkh-ten zee gairn toon*
Do you like...?	Mögen Sie...? *mur-gen zee*

YOU MAY HEAR...

Was machen Sie?
vus makhen zee
What do you do?

Sind Sie im Urlaub?
zint zee im oor-lowp
Are you on vacation?

DAYS OF THE WEEK

What day is it today?	Welcher Tag ist heute? *vel-kher tahk ist hoy-te*	**Friday**	Freitag *fry-tahk*
Sunday	Sonntag *zon-tahk*	**Saturday**	Samstag *zums-tahk*
Monday	Montag *mohn-tahk*	**today**	heute *hoy-te*
Tuesday	Dienstag *deens-tahk*	**tomorrow**	morgen *mor-gen*
Wednesday	Mittwoch *mit-vokh*	**yesterday**	gestern *ges-tairn*
Thursday	Donnerstag *don-ners-tahk*	**in...days**	in...Tagen *in...tah-gen*

THE SEASONS

der Frühling
dair frew-ling
spring

der Sommer
dair zom-mer
summer

MONTHS

January	Januar *yunn-oo-ahr*	July	Juli *yoo-lee*
February	Februar *fay-broo-ahr*	August	August *ow-goost*
March	März *mairts*	September	September *zep-tem-bair*
April	April *ah-pril*	October	Oktober *ok-toe-bair*
May	Mai *my*	November	November *no-vem-bair*
June	Juni *yoo-nee*	December	Dezember *day-tsem-bair*

der Herbst
dair hairpst
fall

der Winter
dair vin-ter
winter

ESSENTIALS

TELLING THE TIME 🎧

| What time is it? | Wie spät ist es? |
| | *vee shpayt ist es* |

| It's nine o'clock | Es ist neun Uhr |
| | *es ist noyn oor* |

| ...in the morning | ...morgens |
| | *mor-gens* |

| ...in the afternoon | ...am Nachmittag |
| | *um nakh-mit-tahk* |

| ...in the evening | ...abends |
| | *ah-bents* |

ein Uhr
ine oor
one o'clock

zehn nach eins
tsayn nakh ines
ten past one

Viertel nach eins
feer-tel nakh ines
quarter past one

zwanzig nach eins
tsvun-tsik nakh ines
twenty past one

halb zwei
hulp tsvy
half past one

Viertel vor zwei
feer-tel for tsvy
quarter to two

zehn
vor zwei
tsayn for tsvy
ten to two

zwei Uhr
tsvy oor
two o'clock

It's noon/midnight	**Es ist Mittag/Mitternacht** *es ist mit-tahk/mit-ter-nakht*
second	**die Sekunde** *dee ze-koon-de*
minute	**die Minute** *dee mee-noo-te*
hour	**die Stunde** *dee shtoon-de*
a quarter of an hour	**eine Viertelstunde** *ine-e feer-tel-shtoon-de*
half an hour	**die halbe Stunde** *dee hul-be shtoon-de*
three-quarters of an hour	**die Dreiviertelstunde** *dee dry-feer-tel-shtoon-de*
late	**spät** *shpayt*
early/soon	**früh/bald** *frew/bahlt*
What time does it start?	**Wann beginnt es?** *vun be-ginnt es*
What time does it finish?	**Wann endet es?** *vun en-det es*
How long will it last?	**Wie lange wird es dauern?** *vee lun-ghe veert es dow-ern*

YOU MAY HEAR...

Bis später
bis shpay-ter
See you later

Sie sind früh dran
zee zint frew drun
You're early

Sie sind spät dran
zee zint shpayt drun
You're late

THE WEATHER

What's the weather like?	Wie ist das Wetter? *vee ist dus vet-ter*
It's...	Es ist... *es ist*
...good	...schön *shurn*
...bad	...schlecht *shlekht*
...warm	...warm *varm*
...hot	...heiß *hys*
...cold	...kalt *kult*
...humid	...schwül *shvewl*

Es ist sonnig
es ist zon-nik
It's sunny

Es regnet
es reg-net
It's raining

Es ist wolkig
es ist vol-kik
It's cloudy

Es ist stürmisch
es ist shtewr-mish
It's stormy

What's the forecast?	Wie ist der Wetterbericht? *vee ist dair vet-ter-be-rikht*
What's the temperature?	Wie viele Grad ist es? *vee fee-le graht ist es*
It's...degrees	Es ist...Grad *es ist...graht*
It's a beautiful day	Es ist ein schöner Tag *es ist ine shur-ner tahk*
The weather's changing	Es ist veränderlich *es ist fair-en-der-likh*
Is it going to get colder/ hotter?	Wird es kälter/wärmer? *veert es kel-ter/vehr-mer*
It's cooling down	Es kühlt ab *es kewlt up*
Is it going to freeze?	Wird es eisig? *veert es eye-zik*

Es schneit
es shnyt
It's snowing

Es ist eisig
es ist eye-zik
It's icy

Es ist neblig
es ist neb-lik
It's misty

Es ist
windig
es ist vin-dik
It's windy

GETTING AROUND

Germany has an excellent road and highway (*Autobahn*)
system if you are traveling around the country by car.
German trains are fast and punctual, linking the main
urban centres. In larger towns and cities, you can usually
get around by taxi or through the integrated transport
system of trams, buses and, sometimes, subways
(*U-Bahn*). All you need to do is to buy a ticket
in advance and then validate it when you travel.

ASKING WHERE THINGS ARE

Excuse me, please	**Entschuldigen Sie, bitte** *ent-shool-di-gen zee bit-te*
Where is...	**Wo ist...** *vo ist*
...the town center?	**...das Stadtzentrum?** *dus shtut-tsen-troom*
...the train station?	**...der Bahnhof?** *dair bahn-hohf*
...a cash machine?	**...ein Geldautomat?** *ine gelt-ow-toe-mat*
How do I get to...?	**Wie komme ich zu...?** *vee kom-me ikh tsoo*
I'm going to the train station	**Ich gehe zum Bahnhof** *ikh gay-e tsoom bahn-hohf*
I'm looking for a restaurant	**Ich suche nach einem Restaurant** *ikh zookhe nahkh ine-em res-to-rung*
I'm lost	**Ich habe mich verlaufen** *ikh hah-be mikh fair-low-fen*
Is it near?	**Ist es in der Nähe?** *ist es in dair nay-he*
Is there a bank nearby?	**Ist eine Bank in der Nähe?** *ist ine-e bunk in dair nay-he*
Is it far?	**Ist es weit?** *ist es vyte*
How far is...	**Wie weit ist es...** *vee vyte ist es*
...the town hall?	**...zum Rathaus?** *tsoom raht-hows*
...the market?	**...zum Markt?** *tsoom markt*
Can I walk there?	**Kann ich zu Fuß hingehen?** *kunn ikh tsoo foos hin-gay-en*

CAR AND BIKE RENTAL

Where is the car rental desk?	**Wo ist der Mietwagenschalter?** *vo ist dair meet-vahgen-shal-ter*
I want to rent...	**Ich möchte...mieten** *ikh murkh-te...mee-ten*
...a car	**...ein Auto** *ine ow-toe*
...a motorcycle	**...ein Motorrad** *ine mo-tor-raht*
...a bicycle	**...ein Fahrrad** *ine far-raht*
...for...days	**...für...Tage** *fewr...tah-ge*
...for a week	**...für eine Woche** *fewr ine-e vo-khe*

die Limousine
dee lee-mo-zee-ne
sedan

das Hecktürmodell
dus heck-tewr-mo-dell
hatchback

das Motorrad
dus mo-tor-raht
motorcycle

der Motorroller
dair mo-tor-roll-ler
scooter

das Mountainbike
dus mountain-bike
mountain bike

das Rennrad
dus ren-raht
road bike

...for the weekend	...für das Wochenende *fewr dus vo-khen-end-e*
I'd like...	Ich möchte... *ikh murkh-te*
...an automatic	...einen Wagen mit Automatikgetriebe *ine-en vahgen mit ow-toe-matik-ge-tree-be*
...a manual	...einen Wagen mit Handschaltung *ine-en vahgen mit hunt-shal-tung*
Has it got air-conditioning?	Hat er eine Klimaanlage? *hut air ine-e kleema-an-lahge*
Should I return it with a full tank?	Soll ich den Wagen vollgetankt zurückbringen? *zoll ikh dain vahgen foll-ge-tunkt tsoo-rewk-brin-gen*
Here's my driver's license	Hier ist mein Führerschein *heer ist mine few-rer-shine*
Do you have a bicycle?	Haben Sie ein Fahrrad? *hah-ben zee ine far-raht*

der Fahrradhelm
dair far-raht-helm
cycling helmet

die Fahrradpumpe
dee far-raht-poom-pe
bicycle pump

das Fahrradschloss
dus far-raht-shlos
lock

der Kindersitz
dair kin-der-zits
child seat

DRIVING

Is this the road to the station?	**Ist das die Straße zum Banhnhof?** *ist dus dee shtrah-se tsoom bahn-hohf*
Where is the nearest garage?	**Wo ist die nächste Werkstatt?** *vo ist dee nekh-ste vairk-stut*
I'd like...	**Ich hätte gern...** *ikh het-te gairn*
...some gas	**...etwas Benzin** *et-vas ben-tseen*
...40 liters of unleaded	**...40 Liter Bleifrei** *feer-tsik lee-ter bly-fry*
...30 liters of diesel	**...30 Liter Diesel** *dry-sik lee-ter dee-zel*
Fill it up, please	**Volltanken, bitte** *foll-tun-ken bit-te*
Where do I pay?	**Wo kann ich zahlen?** *vo kunn ikh tsah-len*
The pump number is...	**Die Nummer der Zapfsäule ist...** *dee noo-mer dair tsapf-zoyle ist*
Can I pay by credit card?	**Kann ich mit Kreditkarte zahlen?** *kunn ikh mit kray-deet-kar-te tsah-len*
Please can you check...	**Könnten Sie bitte...prüfen** *kurn-ten zee bit-te...prew-fen*
...the oil	**...das Öl** *dus url*
...the tire pressure	**...den Reifendruck** *den rye-fen-drook*

PARKING

Is there a parking lot nearby?	**Ist ein Parkplatz in der Nähe?** *ist ine park-pluts in dair nay-he*
Can I park here?	**Kann ich hier parken?** *kunn ikh heer par-ken*
How long can I park for?	**Wie lange kann ich parken?** *vee lun-ge kunn ikh par-ken*
Is it free?	**Ist er gratis?** *ist air gra-tis*
How much does it cost?	**Wie viel kostet es?** *vee feel kos-tet es*
How much is it...	**Wie viel kostet es...** *vee feel kos-tet es*
...per hour?	**...pro Stunde?** *pro shtoon-de*
...per day?	**...pro Tag?** *pro tahk*
...overnight?	**...über Nacht?** *ew-ber nakht*

der Dachgepäckträger
dair dakh-ge-pek-trayger
roofrack

der Kindersitz
dair kin-der-zits
child seat

die Tankstelle
dee tunk-shtel-le
gas station

THE CAR

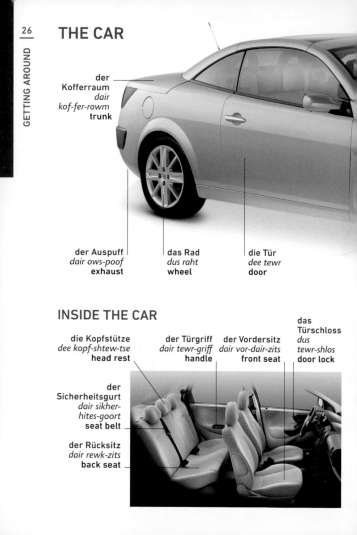

der
Kofferraum
*dair
kof-fer-rowm*
trunk

der Auspuff
dair ows-poof
exhaust

das Rad
dus raht
wheel

die Tür
dee tewr
door

INSIDE THE CAR

die Kopfstütze
dee kopf-shtew-tse
head rest

der Türgriff
dair tewr-griff
handle

der Vordersitz
dair vor-dair-zits
front seat

das
Türschloss
*dus
tewr-shlos*
door lock

der
Sicherheitsgurt
*dair sikher-
hites-goort*
seat belt

der Rücksitz
dair rewk-zits
back seat

die Windschutzscheibe
dee vint-shoots-shy-be
windshield

die Motorhaube
dee mo-tor-how-be
hood

der Scheinwerfer
dair shyn-vair-fer
headlight

die Stoßstange
dee shtows-shtange
bumper

der Reifen
dair rye-fen
tire

der Motor
dair mo-tor
engine

THE CONTROLS

das Autoradio
dus ow-toe-rah-deeoh
car stereo

die Warnblinkleuchte
dee varn-blink-loykhte
hazard lights

der Tachometer
dair takho-metair
speedometer

der Airbag
dair air-bag
airbag

das Armaturenbrett
dus arma-tooren-bret
dashboard

die Heizung
dee hy-tsoong
heater

die Hupe
dee hoo-pe
horn

der Schalthebel
dair shult-hay-bel
gear shift

das Lenkrad
dus lenk-raht
steering wheel

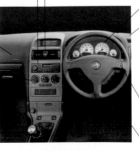

ROAD SIGNS

die Einbahnstraße
dee ine-bahn-shtrah-se
one way

der Kreisverkehr
dair krys-fair-kair
traffic circle

Vorfahrt beachten
for-fart be-akh-ten
yield

Einfahrt verboten
ine-fart fair-bo-ten
no entry

Rechtsabbiegen verboten
rekhts-up-bee-gen fair-bo-ten
no right turn

Parken verboten
par-ken fair-bo-ten
no parking

Anhalten verboten
un-hul-ten fair-bo-ten
no stopping

Gefahr
ge-far
hazard

die Geschwindigkeitsbegrenzung
dee ge-shvindik-kyts-be-grentsoong
speed limit

ON THE ROAD

die Parkuhr
dee park-oor
parking meter

die Verkehrsampel
dee fair-kairs-um-pel
traffic light

der Verkehrspolizist
dair fairkairs-polit-sist
traffic police officer

der Stau
dair shtow
traffic jam

die Straßenkarte
dee shtra-sen-kar-te
map

der Behindertenparkplatz
dair be-hin-der-ten-park-pluts
disabled parking

die Autobahn
dee ow-toe-bahn
highway

die Zubringerstraße
dee tsoo-brin-ger-shtrah-se
entrance/exit ramp

die Notrufsäule
dee not-roof-zoy-le
emergency phone

AT THE STATION

Where can I buy a ticket?	Wo kann ich eine Fahrkarte kaufen? *voe kunn ikh ine-e far-kar-te kow-fen*
Is there an automatic ticket machine?	Gibt es hier einen Fahrscheinautomaten? *geept es heer ine-en far-shine-owtoe-maten*
How much is a ticket to...?	Was kostet eine Fahrkarte nach...? *vus kos-tet ine-e far-kar-te nakh*
Two tickets to...	Zwei Fahrkarten nach... *tsvy far-kar-ten nakh*
I'd like...	Ich möchte... *ikh murkh-te*
...a one-way ticket to...	...eine einfache Fahrkarte nach... *ine-e ine-fakhe far-kar-te nakh*
...a return ticket to...	...eine Rückfahrkarte nach... *ine-e rewk-far-kar-te nakh*
...a first-class ticket	...eine Fahrkarte erster Klasse *ine-e far-kar-te air-ster kluss-se*
...a standard-class ticket	...eine normale Fahrkarte *ine-e nor-mah-le far-kar-te*

der Fahrscheinautomat
dair far-shine-owtoe-mat
automatic ticket machine

die Fahrkarte
dee far-kar-te
ticket

I'd like to...	Ich möchte gern... *ikh murkh-te gairn*
...reserve a seat	...einen Sitzplatz reservieren *ine-en zits-pluts re-zair-vee-ren*
...on the ICE to...	...mit dem ICE nach... *mit daim ee-tseh-ay nakh*
...book a sleeper berth	...einen Liegeplatz reservieren *ine-nen lee-ge-pluts re-zair-vee-ren*
Is there a reduction...?	Gibt es eine Ermäßigung...? *geept es ine-e er-mess-i-goong*
...for children?	...für Kinder? *fewr kin-der*
...for students?	...für Studenten? *fewr shtoo-den-ten*
...for senior citizens?	...für Senioren? *fewr Ze-nee-o-ren*
Is it a fast train?	Ist es ein schneller Zug? *ist es ine shnel-ler tsook*
Do I stamp the ticket before boarding?	Muss ich die Fahrkarte vor dem Einsteigen entwerten? *moos ikh dee far-kar-te for daim ine-shty-gen ent-vair-ten*

YOU MAY HEAR...

Der Zug fährt von Bahnsteig...ab
dair tsook fairt fon bahn-shtyk...up
The train leaves from platform...

TRAVELING BY TRAIN

Do you have a timetable?	**Haben Sie einen Fahrplan?** *hah-ben zee ine-en far-plun*
What time is...	**Wann fährt...** *vun fairt*
...the next train to...?	**...der nächste Zug nach...?** *dair nekh-ste tsook nakh*
...the last train to...?	**...der letzte Zug nach...?** *dair lets-te tsook nakh*
Which platform does it leave from?	**Von welchem Bahnsteig fährt er ab?** *fon vel-khem bahn-shtyk fairt air up*
What time does it arrive in...?	**Wann kommt er in...an?** *vun komt air in...un*
How long does it take?	**Wie lange dauert die Fahrt?** *vee lan-ge dow-ert dee fart*
Is this the train for...?	**Ist das der Zug nach...?** *ist das dair tsook nakh*
Is this the right platform for...?	**Ist das der richtige Bahnsteig für...?** *ist das dair rickh-ti-ge bahn-shtyk fewr*
Where is platform three?	**Wo ist Bahnsteig drei?** *vo ist bahn-shtyk dry*

YOU MAY HEAR...

Sie müssen Ihren Fahrschein entwerten
zee mew-sen eer-en far-shine ent-vair-ten
You must validate your ticket

Benutzen Sie die Maschine
be-noot-sen zee dee ma-shee-ne
Use the machine

Does this train stop at...?	Hält dieser Zug in...? *helt deezer tsook in*
Where do I change for...?	Wo muss ich nach...umsteigen? *vo moos ikh nakh...oom-shtygen*
Is this seat free?	Ist dieser Platz noch frei? *ist deezer pluts nokh fry*
I've reserved this seat	Ich habe diesen Platz reserviert *ikh hah-be deezen pluts re-zair-veert*
Do I get off here?	Muss ich hier aussteigen? *moos ikh heer ows-shtygen*
Where is the subway station?	Wo ist die U-Bahnstation? *vo ist dee oo-bahn-shta-tsee-on*
Which line goes to...?	Welche Linie fährt nach...? *vel-khe lee-nee-e fairt nakh*

die Bahnhofshalle
dee bahn-hohfs-hull-le
concourse

der Zug
dair tsook
train

der Speisewagen
dair shpy-ze-vahgen
dining car

der Liegeplatz
dair lee-ge-pluts
sleeper berth

BUSES

When is the next bus to the town center?

Wann fährt der nächste Bus zum Stadtzentrum?
vun fairt dair nekh-ste boos tsoom shtut-tsen-troom

What is the fare to the airport?

Was kostet die Fahrt zum Flughafen?
vus kos-tet dee fart tsoom flook-hah-fen

Where is the nearest bus stop?

Wo ist die nächste Bushaltestelle?
vo ist dee nekh-ste boos-hul-te-shtel-le

Is this the bus stop for...?

Ist das die Haltestelle für den Bus in Richtung...?
ist dus dee hul-te-shtel-le fewr dain boos in rikh-toong

Does the number 4 stop here?

Hält der Bus Nummer 4 hier an?
helt dair boos noom-mer feer heer un

Where can I buy a ticket?

Wo kann ich einen Fahrschein kaufen?
vo kunn ikh ine-nen far-shine kow-fen

Can I pay on the bus?

Kann ich im Bus zahlen?
kunn ikh im boos tsah-len

Which buses go to the city center?

Welche Busse fahren ins Stadtzentrum?
vel-khe boos-se fah-ren ins shtut-tsen-troom

der Bus
dair boos
bus

der Busbahnhof
dair boos-bahn-hohf
bus station

TAXIS

Where can I get a taxi?	**Wo kann ich ein Taxi nehmen?** *vo kunn ikh ine tuck-see nay-men*
Can I order a taxi?	**Kann ich ein Taxi bestellen?** *kunn ikh ine tuck-see be-stel-len*
Can you take me to the library?	**Könnten Sie mich zur Bibliothek fahren?** *kurn-ten zee mikh tsoor bib-lee-o-tayk fah-ren*
Is it far?	**Ist es weit weg?** *ist es vyte vek*
How long will it take?	**Wie lange wird es dauern?** *vee lan-ge veert es dow-ern*
How much will it cost?	**Was kostet die Fahrt?** *vus kos-tet dee fart*
Can you drop me here?	**Können sie mich hier absetzen?** *kur-nen zee mikh heer up-zet-sen*
What do I owe you?	**Was schulde ich Ihnen?** *vus shool-de ikh een-en*
I don't have any change	**Ich habe kein Kleingeld** *ikh ha-be kine kline-gelt*
Please, may I have a receipt?	**Kann ich bitte eine Quittung haben?** *kunn ikh bi-te ine-e kvit-toong hah-ben*

das Taxi
dus tuck-see
taxi

BOATS

Are there any boat trips?	**Gibt es Schifffahrten?** *gee-pt es shif-far-ten*
Where does the boat leave from?	**Wo fährt das Schiff ab?** *vo fairt dus shif up*
When is...	**Wann fährt...?** *vun fairt*
...the next boat to...?	**...das nächste Schiff nach...?** *dus nekh-ste shif nakh*
...the first boat?	**...das erste Schiff?** *dus airs-te shif*
...the last boat?	**...das letzte Schiff?** *dus lets-te shif*
I'd like two tickets for...	**Ich möchte zwei Fahrkarten für...** *ikh murkh-te tsvy far-kar-ten fewr*
...the cruise	**...die Rundfahrt** *dee roont-fart*

die Fähre
dee fai-re
ferry

das Tragflügelboot
dus truk-flew-gel-boht
hydrofoil

die Jacht
dee yakht
yacht

das Hovercraft
dus hover-kraft
hovercraft

...the river trip	...die Flussfahrt *dee floos-fart*
How much is it for...	Was kostet es für...? *vus kos-tet es fewr*
...a car and two people?	...ein Auto und zwei Passagiere? *ine ow-toe oont tsvy passa-sheer-e*
...a family?	...eine Familie? *ine-e fa-mee-lee-ye*
...a cabin	...eine Kabine? *ine-e kah-bee-ne*
Can I buy a ticket on board?	Kann ich eine Fahrkarte an Bord kaufen? *kunn ikh ine-e far-kar-te un bort kow-fen*
Is there wheelchair access?	Gibt es Zugang für Rollstuhlfahrer? *geept es tsoo-gung fewr roll-shtool-fah-rer*

das Ausflugsschiff
dus ows-flewks-shif
pleasure boat

der
Rettungsring
*dair ret-
toongs-ring*
life ring

der Katamaran
dair ka-ta-ma-run
catamaran

die
Schwimmweste
dee shvim-ves-te
life jacket

AIR TRAVEL

Which terminal do I need?	**Welches ist mein Terminal?** *vel-khes ist mine tair-mi-nal*
What time do I check in?	**Wann ist der Check-in?** *van ist dair check-in*
Where is...	**Wo ist...** *vo ist*
...the arrivals hall?	**...die Ankunftshalle?** *dee un-koonfts-hull-le*
...the departures hall?	**...die Abflughalle?** *dee up-flook-hull-le*
...the boarding gate?	**...das Gate?** *dus gate*
Where do I check in?	**Wo muss ich einchecken?** *vo moos ikh ine-check-en*
I'm traveling...	**Ich reise in...** *ikh rye-ze in*
...economy	**...der Economy-Class** *dair economy class*
...business class	**...der Business-Class** *dair business class*

die Reisetasche
dee ry-ze-tu-she
duffel bag

der Pass
dair pus
passport

die Bordmahlzeit
dee bort-mahl-tsyt
in-flight meal

die Bordkarte
dee bort-kar-te
boarding pass

Here is my passport	**Hier ist mein Pass** *heer ist mine pus*
I have an e-ticket	**Ich habe ein E-Ticket** *ikh hah-be ine ee-ticket*
I'm checking in one suitcase	**Ich checke einen Koffer ein** *ikh chek-ke ine-nen kof-fer ine*
I packed it myself	**Ich habe ihn selbst gepackt** *ikh hah-be een zelpst ge-pukt*
I have one piece of hand luggage	**Ich habe ein Stück Handgepäck** *ikh hah-be ine shtewk hunt-ge-pek*
What is the weight allowance?	**Wie hoch ist die Gewichtszulassung?** *vee hokh ist dee ge-vikhst-tsoo-lus-soong*
How much is excess baggage?	**Was kostet das Übergepäck?** *vus kos-tet das ew-ber-ge-pek*
I'd like...	**Ich hätte gern...** *ikh het-te gairn*
...a window seat	**...einen Fensterplatz** *ine-nen fen-ster-pluts*
...an aisle seat	**...einen Gangplatz** *ine-nen gung-pluts*

YOU MAY HEAR...

Ihren Pass/Ihren Flugschein, bitte
ee-ren pus/ee-ren flook-shine bit-te
Your passport/ticket please

Ist das ihre Tasche?
ist dus ee-re tu-she
Is this your bag?

AT THE AIRPORT

| Here's my... | Hier ist... |
| | *heer ist* |

| ...boarding pass | ...meine Bordkarte |
| | *my-ne bort-kar-te* |

| ...passport | ...mein Pass |
| | *mine pus* |

| Can I change some money? | Kann ich Geld wechseln? |
| | *kunn ikh gelt vek-zeln* |

| What is the exchange rate? | Wie ist der Wechselkurs? |
| | *vee ist dair vek-sel-koors* |

| Is the flight delayed? | Hat der Flug Verspätung? |
| | *hut dair flook fair-shpay-toong* |

| How late is it? | Wie spät ist es? |
| | *vee shpayt ist es* |

der Check-In-Schalter
dair check-in-shul-ter
check-in

der Währungsumtausch
dair vay-roongs-oom-towsh
currency exchange booth

die Passkontrolle
dee pus-kon-troll-le
passport control

der Duty-Free-Shop
dair duty-free-shop
duty-free shop

die Gepäckausgabe
dee ge-pek-ows-gah-be
baggage claim

der Pilot
dair pee-loht
pilot

das Flugzeug
dus flook-tsoyk
airplane

die Flugbegleiterin
dee flook-be-gly-tair-in
flight attendant

Which gate does flight... leave from?	**Von welchem Gate geht der Flug...ab?** *fon vel-khem gate gayt dair flook...up*
What time do I board?	**Wann gehe ich an Bord?** *vunn gay-e ikh un bort*
When does the gate close?	**Wann schließt das Gate?** *vun shleest dus gate*
Where are the carts?	**Wo sind die Gepäckwagen?** *vo zint dee ge-pek-vah-gen*
Here is the baggage claim tag	**Hier ist das Gepäcketikett** *heer ist dus ge-pek-eti-ket*
I can't find my baggage	**Ich kann mein Gepäck nicht finden** *ikh kunn mine ge-pek nikht fin-den*
My baggage hasn't arrived	**Mein Gepäck ist nicht angekommen** *mine ge-pek ist nikht un-ge-kom-men*

EATING OUT

German, Austrian, and Swiss food tends to be hearty and appetizing. You can choose from cafés and bars (*Weinstube*), which serve a variety of drinks and snacks, as well as traditional restaurants (*Gasthöfe*) serving local specialties, and larger more international eateries (*Gaststätte*). German beer is especially delicious and justly famous, and every area has its own special brew, which you can sample in *Bierkeller* and *Biergärten*.

MAKING A RESERVATION

I'd like...	Ich möchte... *ikh murkh-te*
...to book a table for lunch/dinner	...einen Tisch zum Mittagessen/ Abendessen *ine-nen tish tsoom mit-takh-es-sen/ ah-bent-es-sen*
...to book a table for four people	...einen Tisch für vier Personen reservieren *ine-nen tish fewr feer per-zoe-nen re-zair-vee-ren*
...to book a table for this evening	...einen Tisch für heute Abend reservieren *ine-nen tish fewr hoy-te ah-bent re-zair-vee-ren*
...to book a table for tomorrow at one	...einen Tisch für morgen dreizehn Uhr reservieren *ine-nen tish fewr mor-gen dry-tsayn oor re-zair-vee-ren*
Do you have a table earlier/later?	Haben Sie einen Tisch früher/später? *hah-ben zee ine-nen tish frew-er/shpay-ter*
My name is...	Mein Name ist... *mine nah-me ist*
My telephone number is...	Meine Telefonnummer ist... *my-ne tay-lay-foen-noom-mer ist*
Do you take credit cards?	Nehmen Sie Kreditkarten? *nay-men zee kray-deet-kar-ten*
I have a reservation	Ich habe eine Reservierung *ikh hah-be ine-e re-zair-vee-roong*
in the name of...	auf den Namen... *owf dain nah-men*
We haven't booked	Wir haben nicht reserviert *veer hah-ben nikht re-zair-veert*

ORDERING A MEAL

May we see the menu?	Können wir die Speisekarte sehen? *kur-nen veer dee shpy-ze-kar-te zay-hen*
...see the wine list?	...die Weinkarte sehen? *dee vine-kar-te zay-hen*
Do you have...	Haben Sie... *hah-ben zee*
...a set menu?	...ein Tagesmenü? *ine tah-ges-menew*
...a fixed-price menu?	...ein Festpreismenü? *ine fest-prize-menew*
...a children's menu?	...ein Kindermenü? *ine kin-der-menew*
...an à la carte menu	...ein Menü à la carte? *ine menew à la carte*
What are today's specials?	Welche Spezialgerichte gibt es heute? *vel-khe shpay-tsee-al-ge-rikhte geept es hoy-te*

YOU MAY HEAR...

Haben Sie
reserviert?
*hah-ben zee
re-zair-veert*
**Do you have a
reservation?**

Bitte nehmen
Sie Platz
*bit-te nay-men
zee pluts*
Please be seated

Auf welchen
Namen?
*owf vel-khen
nah-men*
In what name?

Möchten Sie
bestellen?
*murkh-ten zee
be-shtel-len*
**Are you ready
to order?**

What are the local specialties?	Was sind die örtlichen Spezialitäten? *vus zint dee urt-likhen shpay-tsee-al-ee-tay-ten*
What do you recommend?	Was empfehlen Sie? *vus em-pfay-len zee*
What is this?	Was ist das? *vus ist dus*
Are there any vegetarian dishes?	Haben Sie vegetarische Speisen? *hah-ben zee vay-ge-tah-ree-shuh shpy-zen*
I can't ...	Ich kann... *ikh kunn*
...eat dairy foods	...keine Molkereiprodukte essen *kine-e mol-ker-eye-pro-dook-te es-sen*
...eat nuts	...keine Nüsse essen *kine-e news-se es-sen*
...eat wheat	...keinen Weizen essen *kine-nen vy-tsen es-sen*
To start, I'll have...	Als Vorspeise nehme ich... *uls for-shpy-ze nay-me ikh*
To drink, I'll have...	Zum Trinken nehme ich... *tsoom trin-ken nay-me ikh*

READING THE MENU...

Vorspeisen *for-shpy-zen* **appetizers**	**die Hauptspeisen** *dee howpt-shpy-zen* **main courses**	**Käse** *kay-ze* **cheeses**
erster Gang *air-ster gang* **first courses**	**das Gemüse** *dus ge-mew-ze* **vegetables**	**die Nachspeisen** *dee nakh-shpy-zen* **desserts**

COMPLAINING

I didn't order this	Das habe ich nicht bestellt *dus hah-be ikh nikht be-shtelt*
We can't wait any longer	Wir können nicht länger warten *veer kur-nen nikht len-ger var-ten*

PAYING

The check, please	Die Rechnung, bitte *dee rekh-noong bit-te*
Can we pay separately?	Können wir getrennt zahlen? *kur-nen veer ge-trennt tsah-len*
May I...	Kann ich... *kunn ikh*
...have a receipt?	...eine Quittung haben? *ine-e kvit-toong hah-ben*
...have an itemized bill?	...eine detaillierte Rechnung haben? *ine-e day-ty-leer-te rekh-noong hah-ben*
Is service included?	Ist die Bedienung inbegriffen? *ist dee be-dee-noong in-be-griffen*

YOU MAY HEAR...

Wir nehmen keine Kreditkarten
veer nay-men ky-ne kray-deet-kar-ten
We don't take credit cards

Geben Sie bitte Ihre Geheimzahl ein
gay-ben zee bit-te ee-re ge-hime-tsahl ine
Please enter your PIN

DISHES AND CUTLERY

der kleine Teller
dair cly-ne teller
side plate

die Schüssel
dee shew-sel
bowl

das Salz
dus zults
salt

der Pfeffer
dair pfeffer
pepper

der Dessertlöffel
dair des-sair-lurfel
dessert spoon

die Tasse und die Untertasse
dee tuss-e oont dee unter-tuss-e
cup and saucer

das Glas
dus glahs
glass

der Teelöffel
dair teh-lurfel
teaspoon

die Serviette
dee zair-vee-et-te
napkin

die Gabel
dee gah-bel
fork

das Messer
dus mes-ser
knife

der Teller
dair tel-ler
dinner plate

AT THE CAFÉ OR BAR

The menu, please	Die Speisekarte, bitte *dee shpy-ze-kar-te bit-te*
Do you have...?	Haben Sie...? *hah-ben zee*
What fruit juices/ herbal teas do you have?	Welche Fruchtsäfte/Kräutertees haben Sie? *vel-khe frookht-zef-te/kroy-ter-tays* *hah-ben zee*
I'd like...	Ich möchte... *ikh murkh-te*
I'll have...	Ich nehme... *ikh nay-me*

der Kaffee mit Milch
dair kuf-fay mit milkh
coffee with milk

der schwarze Kaffee
dair shvur-tse kuf-fay
black coffee

der Kaffee mit Schlagsahne
dair kuf-fay mit shluk-zah-ne
coffee with whipped cream

YOU MAY HEAR...

Was darf es sein?
vus darf es zine
What would you like?

Möchten Sie noch etwas?
murkh-ten zee nokh et-vus
Anything else?

Gern geschehen
gairn ge-shay-en
You're welcome

der Tee mit Milch
dair tay mit milkh
tea with milk

der Tee mit Zitrone
dair tay mit tsee-troh-ne
tea with lemon

der Pfefferminztee
dair pfef-fer-mints-tay
mint tea

der grüne Tee
dair grew-ne tay
green tea

der Kamillentee
dair kah-mill-len-tay
chamomile tea

die heiße Schokolade
dee hy-se shoko-lah-de
hot chocolate

A bottle of...	Eine Flasche... *ine-e flu-shuh*
A glass of...	Ein Glas... *ine glahs*
A cup of...	Eine Tasse... *ine-e tuss-se*
...with lemon/milk	...mit Zitrone/Milch *mit tsee-troh-ne/milkh*
Another...please	Noch ein/eine...bitte *nokh ine/ine-e...bit-te*
The same again, please	Bitte das gleiche noch einmal *bit-te dus gly-khe nokh ine-mul*

CAFÉ AND BAR DRINKS

der Ananassaft
dair ah-nah-nus-zuft
pineapple juice

der Apfelsaft
dair up-fel-zuft
apple juice

der Orangensaft
dair oh-run-dshen-zuft
orange juice

die Limonade
dee lee-mo-nahde
lemonade

der Traubensaft
dair trow-ben-zuft
grape juice

der Tomatensaft
dair tomah-ten-zuft
tomato juice

der Gin und Tonic
dair gin oont tonic
gin and tonic

die Cola
dee koh-lah
cola

der Eiskaffee
dair ice-kuf-fay
iced coffee

die Apfelschorle
dee up-fel-shorle
sparkling apple juice

das Sodawasser
dus zo-da-vuss-ser
soda water

die Flasche Bier
dee flu-shuh beer
bottle of beer

die Flasche Mineralwasser
dee flu-shuh mee-nair-al-vusser
bottle of mineral water

das Glas Bier
dus glahs beer
glass of beer

die Flasche Weißwein
dee flu-shuh vice-vine
bottle of white wine

das Glas Rotwein
dus glahs roht-vine
glass of red wine

YOU MAY HEAR...

In der Flasche oder vom Fass?
in dair flu-shuh odair fom fuss
Bottled or draft?

Mit oder ohne Kohlensäure?
mit odair oh-ne ko-len-zoyre
Still or sparkling?

Mit Eis?
mit ice
With ice?

BAR SNACKS

das Sandwich
dus zand-wich
sandwich

die Frankfurter mit Senf
dee frunk-foor-ter mit zenf
Frankfurters with mustard

die Currywurst
dee kurry-voorst
curried sausage

die Nüsse
dee newss-se
nuts

die Bratwürstchen
dee brat-vewrst-khen
sausages with potatoes

der Kartoffelsalat
dair kahr-toffel-zah-laht
potato salad

der Kuchen
dair koo-khen
cake

das Plundergebäck
dus ploon-der-gebek
Danish pastry

das Eis
dus ice
ice cream

die Brezeln
dee bray-tseln
pretzels

FAST FOOD

May I have...
   Ich hätte gerne...
   ikh het-te ger-ne

...to eat in/carry out
   ...hier essen/mitnehmen?
   tsoom heer ess-sen/mit-nay-men

...some ketchup/mustard
   ...etwas Ketchup/Senf?
   et-vus ketch-up/zenf

der Hamburger
dair ham-burger
hamburger

der Chickenburger
dair chicken-burger
chicken burger

der Wrap
dair rap
wrap

der Hot Dog
dair hot dog
hot dog

der Kebab
dair keh-bub
kebab

die Pommes
dee pomm-mes
French fries

das Brathähnchen
dus braht-hen-khen
fried chicken

die Pizza
dee peetsa
pizza

BREAKFAST

May I...	Kann ich... *kunn ikh*
...have some sugar	...etwas Zucker haben? *et-vus tsoo-ker hah-ben*
...have some milk	...etwas Milch haben? *et-vus milkh hah-ben*
...have some artificial sweetener	...etwas Süßstoff haben? *et-vus zews-shtoff hah-ben*
...have some butter	...etwas Butter haben? *et-vus boo-ter hah-ben*
...have some jam?	...etwas Marmelade haben? *et-vus mar-meh-lah-de hah-ben*

der Kaffee
dair kuf-fay
coffee

die heiße Schokolade
dee hy-se shoko-lah-de
hot chocolate

der Tee
dair tay
tea

der Orangensaft
dair oh-run-dshen-zuft
orange juice

der Apfelsaft
dair up-fel-zuft
apple juice

das Croissant
dus krwassant
croissant

das Brötchen
dus brurt-khen
bread roll

das Brot
dus broht
bread

der Schinken
dair shin-ken
ham

der Käse
dair kay-ze
cheese

das gekochte Ei
dus ge-kokh-te eye
boiled egg

das pochierte Ei
dus pokheer-te ye
poached egg

der Fruchtjoghurt
dair frewkht-yog-hurt
fruit yogurt

das Rührei
dus ruhr-eye
scrambled eggs

der Honig
dair hoh-nik
honey

das frische Obst
dus free-shuh opst
fresh fruit

FIRST COURSES

die Frittatensuppe
dee frit-tah-ten-zoop-pe
broth with pancake strips

die Fleischbrühe
dee flysh-brew-e
broth

die Kartoffelsuppe
dee kar-toffel-zoop-pe
potato soup

die Rindersuppe
dee rinder-zoop-pe
beef broth

die Suppe
dee zoop-pe
soup

die Brotsuppe
dee broht-zoop-pe
bread soup

der Borscht
dair borsht
beet soup

das Soufflé
dus zoof-lay
soufflé

die Eierspeise
dee eye-er-shpy-ze
scrambled omelet

das Omelett
dus om-lett
omelet

der Eier und Pilzsalat
dair eye-er oont pilts-zah-laht
egg and mushroom salad

der Aufschnitt
dair owf-shnit
cold cuts

der Räucherlachs
dair roy-kher-lukhs
smoked salmon

die Pilze in Aspik
dee pil-tse in us-peek
mushrooms in aspic

die Forelle mit Spargel
*dee for-rell-le
mit shpar-gel*
trout with asparagus

der Räucherschinken
dair roy-kher-shin-ken
cured ham

die gefüllte
Tomate
*dee ge-fewl-te
toh-mah-te*
stuffed tomato

das gefüllte
Gemüse
*dus ge-fewl-te
ge-mew-ze*
**stuffed
vegetables**

der
Heringsalat
*dair
hair-ring-zah-laht*
**pickled herring
salad**

die gegrillten
Garnelen
*dee ge-grill-ten
gar-nay-len*
grilled prawns

MAIN COURSES

I would like...	Ich möchte... *ikh murkh-te*	**...the sausage**	...die Wurst *dee wurst*
...the chicken	...das Hähnchen *dus hen-khen*	**roast**	gebraten *ge-brah-ten*
...the duck	...die Ente *dee en-te*	**baked**	gebacken *ge-buck-en*
...the lamb	...das Lamm *dus lum*	**broiled**	gegrillt *ge-grillt*
...the pork	...das Schweinefleisch *dus shvy-ne-flysh*	**on skewers**	am Spieß *um shpees*
...the beef	...das Rindfleisch *dus rind-flysh*	**barbecued**	gegrillt *ge-grillt*
...the steak	...das Beefsteak *dus beef-steak*	**poached**	pochiert *po-sheert*
...the veal	...das Kalbfleisch *dus kulp-flysh*	**boiled**	gekocht *ge-kokht*
...the liver	...die Leber *dee lay-ber*	**fried**	gebraten *ge-brah-ten*

YOU MAY SEE...

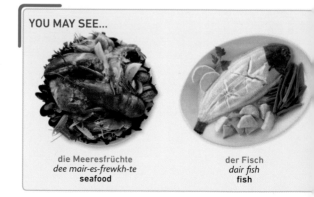

die Meeresfrüchte
dee mair-es-frewkh-te
seafood

der Fisch
dair fish
fish

YOU MAY HEAR...

Wie möchten Sie Ihr Steak?
vee murkh-ten zee eer steak
How do you like your steak?

Englisch, medium oder
durchgebraten?
*eng-lish, mee-dee-um
oh-dair doorkh-ge-brah-ten*
**Rare, medium or
well done?**

pan-fried/ sautéed	kurzgebraten *koorts-ge-brah-ten*	**stewed**	gegart *ge-gart*
stuffed	gefüllt *ge-fewllt*	**with cheese**	mit Käse *mit kay-ze*

das Geflügel
dus ge-flew-gel
poultry

das Fleisch
dus flysh
meat

SALADS AND SIDE DISHES

der grüne Salat
dair grew-ne zah-laht
green salad

das Kartoffelpüree
dus kar-toffel-pew-reh
creamed potato

der gemischte Salat
dair ge-mish-te zah-laht
mixed salad

die Pommes
dee pom-mes
French fries

der Spinat
dair shpee-naht
spinach

der Reis
dair rice
rice

die Nudeln
dee noo-deln
pasta

gedünstetes
Gemüse
*ge-dewns-te-tes
ge-mew-ze*
**steamed
vegetables**

der Rotkohl
dair roht-kohl
red cabbage

das Sauerkraut
dus zower-krowt
sauerkraut

DESSERTS

der Schokoladenpudding
dair shoko-lah-den-poo-ding
chocolate pudding

der Sorbet
dair zor-bay
sherbet

das Speiseeis
dus shpy-ze-ice
ice cream

der Apfelstrudel
dair up-fel-shtroo-del
apple strudel

Berliner mit Mousse
bair-lee-ner mit moos
doughnuts with mousse

die Pfannkuchen
dee pfunn-koo-khen
crêpes

der Kuchen
dair koo-khen
cake

der
Zwetschgendatschi
dair tsvetsh-gen-daht-shee
Bavarian plum tart

die Quarkknödel
dee kvark-knur-del
curd cheese dumplings

die Rote Grütze
dee roh-te grewt-tse
mixed berry compote

PLACES TO STAY

Germany, Austria, and Switzerland have a wide range of
places to stay, depending on your personal preference and
budget. These range from elegant city hotels and historic
Schlösser to smaller, family-run *Pensionen* and traditional
Gasthöfe (country inns). If you prefer self-catering, you can
rent a chalet or apartment, or find a campsite to park your
camper van or put up your tent.

MAKING A RESERVATION

I'd like...	Ich möchte gern... *ikh murkh-te gairn*
...to make a reservation	...ein Zimmer reservieren *ine tsim-mer re-zair-veer-en*
...a double room	...ein Doppelzimmer *ine dop-pel-tsim-mer*
...a room with two twin beds	...ein Zweibettzimmer *ine tsvy-bet-tsim-mer*
...a single room	...ein Einzelzimmer *ine ine-tsel-tsim-mer*
...a family room	...ein Familienzimmer *ine fa-meelee-yen-tsim-mer*
...a disabled person's room	...ein Behindertenzimmer *ine be-hin-dair-ten-tsim-mer*
...with a bathtub/ shower	...mit Bad/Dusche *mit baht/doo-she*
...with a sea view	...mit Blick aufs Meer *mit blik owfs mair*
...for two nights	...für zwei Nächte *fewr tsvy nekh-te*
...for a week	...für eine Woche *fewr ine-e vo-khe*
...from...to...	...von...bis... *...fon...bis...*
Is breakfast included?	Ist das Frühstück inbegriffen? *ist dus frew-shtewk in-be-griffen*
How much is it...	Wie viel kostet es... *vee feel kos-tet es*
...per night?	...pro Nacht? *pro nakht*
...per week?	...pro Woche? *pro vo-khe*

CHECKING IN

I have a reservation in the name of...	Ich habe eine Reservierung auf den Namen... *ikh hah-be ine-e re-zair-vee-rung owf dain nah-men*
Do you have...	Haben Sie...? *hah-ben zee*
I'd like...	Ich hätte gern... *ikh het-te gairn*
...the keys for room...	...die Schlüssel zum Zimmer... *dee shlew-sel tsoom tsim-mer*
...a wake-up call at...	...einen Weckruf um... *ine-nen vek-roof oom*
What time is...	Um wie viel Uhr ist... *oom vee feel oor ist*
...breakfast?	...das Frühstück? *dus frew-shtewk*
...dinner?	...das Abendessen? *dus ah-bent-es-sen*

der Gepäckträger
dair ge-pek-trayger
porter

die Minibar
dee mini-bar
mini bar

der Zimmerservice
dair tsim-mer-service
room service

die Lifte
dee lif-te
elevators

IN YOUR ROOM

Do you have...	Haben Sie... *hah-ben zee*
another...	ein anderes... *ine un-dair-es*
some more...	noch mehr... *nokh mair*

die Decken
dee dek-ken
blankets

die Kopfkissen
dee kopf-kis-sen
pillows

ein Adapter
ine ah-dup-tair
adapter

eine Energiesparlampe
e-ner-ghee-shpah-lam-pe
light bulb

YOU MAY HEAR...

Ihre Zimmernummer ist...
eere tsim-mer-noom-mer ist
Your room number is...

Hier ist Ihr Schlüssel
heer ist eer shlew-sel
Here is your key

IN THE HOTEL 🎧

The room is...	**Das Zimmer ist...** *dus tsim-mer ist*
...too hot	**...zu warm** *tsoo varm*
...too cold	**...zu kalt** *tsoo kult*
...too small	**...zu klein** *tsoo kline*
The window won't open	**Das Fenster lässt sich nicht öffnen** *dus fens-ter lest sikh nikht urf-nen*
The TV doesn't work	**Der Fernseher funktioniert nicht** *dair fairn-zay-er foonk-tsee-yoneert nikht*

der Wasserkocher
dair vus-ser-ko-kher
kettle

der Heizkörper
dair hyts-kur-per
radiator

der Thermostat
dair tair-mo-stat
thermostat

das Einzelzimmer
dus ine-tsel-tsim-mer
single room

das Doppelzimmer
dus dop-pel-tsim-mer
double room

die Zimmernummer
dee tsim-mer-noom-mer
room number

der Fernseher
dair fairn-zay-er
television

die Fernbedienung
dee fairn-be-dee-nung
remote control

der Kleiderbügel
dair kly-der-bew-gel
coat hanger

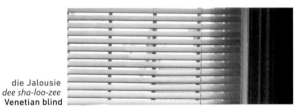

die Jalousie
dee sha-loo-zee
Venetian blind

CHECKING OUT

When do I have to vacate the room?	Wann muss ich das Zimmer freimachen? *van moos ikh dus tsim-mer fry-ma-khen*
May I have the bill, please?	Kann ich bitte die Rechnung haben? *kunn ikh bit-te dee rekh-noong hah-ben*
Can I pay...	Kann ich... *kunn ikh*
...by credit card?	...mit Kreditkarte zahlen? *mit kray-deet-kar-te tsah-len*
...cash?	...bar zahlen? *bar tsah-len*
I'd like a receipt	Ich hätte gern eine Quittung *ikh het-te gairn ine-e kvit-toong*

IN THE BATHROOM

die Handtücher
dee hunt-tewkher
towels

der Bademantel
dair bah-de-mun-tel
bathrobe

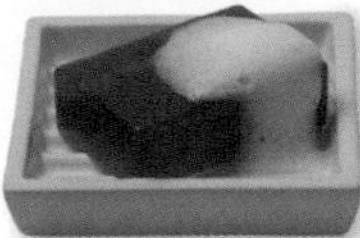

die Seife
dee zy-fe
soap

das Deodorant
dus deo-do-runt
deodorant

die Zahnpasta
dee tsahn-pasta
toothpaste

das Schaumbad
dus showm-baht
bubblebath

das Bidet
dus bee-day
bidet

das Duschgel
dus doosh-gel
shower gel

die Badewanne
dee bah-de-van-ne
bathtub

die Körperlotion
dee kur-per-lo-tsee-on
body lotion

die Zahnbürste
dee tsahn-bewrste
toothbrush

der Föhn
dair furn
blow-dryer

der Rasierapparat
dair rahzeer-uppurat
electric razor

der Rasierschaum
dair rahzeer-showm
shaving foam

das Rasiermesser
dus rahzeer-mes-ser
razor

die Mundspülung
dee moont-shpewloong
mouthwash

das Shampoo
dus sham-poo
shampoo

die Pflegespülung
dee pfle-ge-shpewloong
conditioner

die Nagelschere
dee nah-gel-shair-re
nail clippers

die Nagelschere
dee nah-gel-sheh-re
nail scissors

SELF-CATERING

🎧

May we please...	Könnten wir bitte... *kurn-ten veer bit-te*
...have the key?	...den Schlüssel haben? *dain shlew-sel hah-ben*
...have an extra bed?	...ein Extrabett haben? *ine extra-bet hah-ben*
...have a child's bed?	...ein Kinderbett haben? *ine kin-der-bet hah-ben*
...have more cutlery/ dishes	...mehr Besteck/Geschirr haben? *mair be-shtek/ge-sheer hah-ben*
Where is...	Wo ist... *vo ist*
...the fusebox?	...der Sicherungskasten? *dair zi-kher-oongs-kus-ten*
...the water valve?	...der Absperrhahn? *dair up-shpair-hahn*

der Heizlüfter
dair hyts-lewf-tair
space heater

der Ventilator
dair ven-tee-la-tor
fan

das Gitterbettchen
dus gitter-bet-khen
crib

der Hochstuhl
dair hokh-shtool
high chair

...the nearest doctor?	...der nächste Arzt? *dair nekh-ste artst*
...the supermarket?	...der Supermarkt? *dair zoo-per-markt*
...the nearest store?	...der nächste Laden? *dair nekh-ste lah-den*
Do you do babysitting?	Bieten Sie Kinderbetreuung? *bee-ten zee kin-der-be-troy-oong*
Is there...	Gibt es eine... *geept es ine-e*
...air-conditioning?	...Klimaanlage? *klee-ma-un-lah-ge*
...central heating?	...Zentralheizung? *tsen-tral-hy-tsoong*
How does the heating work?	Wie funktioniert die Heizung? *vee foonk-tsee-yoneert dee hy-tsoong*
When does the cleaner come?	Wann kommt die Reinigungskraft? *vun kommt dee ry-nee-goongs-kruft*
Where do I put the garbage?	Wo kommt der Müll hin? *vo kommt dair mewl hin*
Who do we contact if there are problems?	An wen wenden wir uns bei Problemen? *un vain ven-den veer oons by pro-blay-men*
Do you allow pets?	Sind Haustiere erlaubt? *zint hows-teere air-lowpt*

der Hund
dair hoont
dog

IN THE VILLA

Is there an inventory?

Gibt es eine Inventarliste?
geept es ine-e in-ven-tar-lee-ste

Where is this item?

Wo ist dieser Artikel?
vo ist dee-zer ar-tee-kel

I need...

Ich brauche...
ikh brow-khe

...an adapter

...einen Adapter
ine-nen ah-dup-ter

...an extension cord

...ein Verlängerungskabel
ine fer-len-ger-oongs-kah-bel

...a flashlight

...eine Taschenlampe
ine-e tush-en-lum-pe

die Mikrowelle
dee mee-kro-vell-le
microwave

das Bügeleisen
dus bew-gel-eye-zen
iron

das Bügelbrett
dus bew-gel-bret
ironing board

**der Wischmopp
und Eimer**
*dair vish-mop
oont eye-mer*
mop and bucket

**das Kehrblech/der
Handbesen**
*dus kair-blekh/dair
hunt-bay-zen*
dustpan/brush

das Waschpulver
dus vush-pool-fer
detergent

PROBLEM SOLVING

The shower doesn't work	Die Dusche funktioniert nicht *dee doo-she foonk-tsee-yoneert nikht*
Can you fix it today?	Können Sie das heute reparieren? *kurn-nen zee dus hoy-te re-pah-ree-ren*
There's...	Es gibt... *es geept*
...no electricity	...keinen Strom *kine-nen shtrom*
...no water	...kein Wasser *kine vus-ser*

die Waschmaschine
dee vush-mah-shee-ne
washing machine

der Gefrierkühlschrank
dair ge-freer-kewl-shrunk
side-by-side refrigerator

der Feuerlöscher
dair foy-er-lursher
fire extinguisher

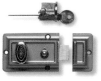

das Schloss und
der Schlüssel
*dus shlos oont
dair shlew-sel*
lock and key

der Rauchmelder
dair rowkh-melder
smoke alarm

der Mülleimer
dair mewl-eye-mer
trash can

KITCHEN EQUIPMENT

das Hackbrett
dus huk-bret
cutting board

das Backblech
dus buk-blekh
cookie sheet

der Rührbesen
dair rewr-bay-zen
whisk

das Küchenmesser
dus kew-khen-mes-ser
kitchen knife

der Gemüseschäler
dair ge-mew-ze-shay-ler
peeler

der Dosenöffner
dair doh-zen-urf-ner
can opener

der Flaschenöffner
dair flu-shen-urf-ner
bottle opener

der Korkenzieher
dair kor-ken-tsee-her
corkscrew

das Reibeisen
dus ribe-eye-zen
grater

der Kochlöffel
dair kokh-lurfel
wooden spoon

die Bratpfanne
dee brut-pfan-ne
frying pan

das Sieb
dus zeeb
colander

der Schaber
dair shah-ber
spatula

der Stieltopf
dair shteel-topf
saucepan

die Grillpfanne
dee grill-pfan-ne
griddle pan

der Schmortopf
dair shmor-topf
casserole dish

die Rührschüssel
dee rewr-shew-sel
mixing bowl

die Schürze
dee shewr-tse
apron

der Topflappen
dair topf-lappen
oven mitts

der Mixer
dair mixer
blender

PLACES TO STAY

CAMPING

Where is the nearest...	Wo ist der nächste... *vo ist dair nekh-ste*
...campsite?	...Campingplatz? *kam-ping-pluts*
...camper van site?	...Wohnwagenplatz? *vohn-vah-gen-pluts*
Do you have any vacancies?	Sind hier Plätze frei? *zint heer plet-se fry*
What is the charge...	Wie viel kostet es... *vee-feel kos-tet es*
...per night?	...pro Nacht? *pro nakht*
...per week?	...pro Woche? *pro vo-khe*
Does the price...	Ist im Preis... *ist im prize*
...include electricity?	...der Strom inbegriffen? *dair shtrohm in-be-griffen*
...include hot water?	...das warme Wasser inbegriffen? *dus var-me vas-ser in-be-griffen*
We want to stay for...	Wir möchten...bleiben *veer murkh-ten...bly-ben*
Can I...	Kann ich... *kunn ikh*

das Zelt
dus tselt
tent

die Zeltspannleine
dee tselt-shpun-lye-ne
guy rope

der Hering
dair hair-ring
tent peg

...rent a tent?	...ein Zelt mieten?	*ine tselt mee-ten*
...rent a bicycle?	...ein Fahrrad mieten?	*ine far-raht mee-ten*
...rent a barbecue?	...einen Grill mieten?	*ine-nen grill mee-ten*
Where are...	Wo sind...	*vo zint*
...the restrooms?	...die Toiletten?	*dee twah-let-ten*
...the garbage cans?	...die Mülltonnen?	*dee mewl-ton-nen*
Are there...	Gibt es...	*geept es*
...showers?	...Duschen?	*doo-shen*
...laundry facilities?	...eine Waschküche?	*ine-e vash-kew-khe*
Is there...	Gibt es...	*geept es*
...a swimming pool?	...ein Schwimmbad?	*ine shvim-baht*
...a store?	...einen Laden?	*ine-nen lah-den*

YOU MAY HEAR...

Feuer sind nicht erlaubt	Das Wasser ist nicht trinkbar
foy-er zint nikht er-lowpt	*dus vuss-ser ist nikht trink-bar*
Don't light a fire	**Don't drink the water**

AT THE CAMPSITE

der Picknickkorb
dair pick-nick-korp
picnic basket

die Thermosflasche
dee tair-mos-fla-shuh
vacuum flask

der Campingkessel
dair kam-ping-kes-sel
camping kettle

die Regenbekleidung
dee ray-gen-be-kly-doong
slickers

das Flaschenwasser
dus flu-shen-vus-ser
bottled water

der Campingkocher
dair kam-ping-ko-kher
camping stove

die Kühltasche
dee kewl-tush-e
cooler

der Grill
dair grill
barbecue

die Luftmatratze
dee looft-mah-trat-se
air mattress

der Schlafsack
dair shlaf-zuck
sleeping bag

die Taschenlampe
dee tu-shen-lum-pe
flashlight

der Rucksack
dair rook-zuck
backpack

der Eimer
dair eye-mer
bucket

der Holzhammer
dair holts-ham-mer
mallet

das Insektenschutzmittel
dus in-zek-ten-shoots-mittel
insect repellent

das Sonnenschutzmittel
dus zon-nen-shoots-mittel
sunscreen

das Pflaster
dus pflus-ter
adhesive bandage

der Schnurknäuel
dair shnoor-knoy-el
ball of string

die Wanderstiefel
dee vun-der-shtee-fel
hiking boots

der Kompass
dair kom-puss
compass

SHOPPING

As well as department stores, supermarkets, and specialist shops, Germany has many picturesque open-air markets in town squares and on high streets, where you can buy food, clothes, and even antiques relatively cheaply. Most shops are open between 9.00am and 6–8.00pm Monday to Friday. Note that many close at 4.00pm on Saturdays. Weekly markets (*Wochenmärkte*) are often held on Saturdays in many towns.

IN THE STORE

I'm looking for...	Ich suche nach... *ikh zoo-khe nakh*
Do you have...?	Haben Sie...? *hah-ben zee*
I'm just looking	Ich sehe mich nur um *ikh zay-he mikh noor oom*
I'm being served	Ich werde schon bedient *ikh vair-de shon be-deent*
Do you have any more of these?	Haben Sie noch mehr von diesen? *hah-ben zee nokh mair fon dee-zen*
How much is this?	Wie viel kostet das? *vee feel kos-tet dus*
Have you anything cheaper?	Haben Sie etwas Billigeres? *hah-ben zee et-vus bee-lee-ger-es*
I'll take this one	Ich nehme dieses *ikh nay-me dee-zes*
Where can I pay?	Wo kann ich zahlen? *vo kunn ikh tsah-len*
I'll pay...	Ich zahle... *ikh tsah-le*
...in cash	...bar *bar*
...by credit card	...mit Kreditkarte *mit kray-deet-kar-te*
May I have a receipt?	Kann ich eine Quittung haben? *kunn ikh ine-e kvit-toong hah-ben*
I'd like to exchange this	Ich möchte das gern umtauschen *ikh murkh-te dus gairn oom-tow-shen*

IN THE BANK

I'd like...	Ich möchte... *ikh murkh-te*
...to make a withdrawal	...Geld abheben *gelt up-hay-ben*
...to deposit some money	...Geld einzahlen *gelt ine-tsah-len*
...to change some money	...Geld wechseln *gelt vek-seln*
...into euros	...in Euro *in oy-roe*
...into dollars/sterling	...in Dollars/britische Pfund *in dollahrs/brit-tishe pfoont*
Here is my passport	Hier ist mein Pass *heer ist mine pahs*
My name is...	Ich heiße... *ikh hys-se*
My account number is...	Meine Kontonummer ist... *my-ne kon-toe-noo-mer ist*
My bank details are...	Meine Bankangaben lauten... *my-ne bunk-un-gah-ben low-ten*

der Pass
dair pus
passport

das Geld
dus gelt
money

der Wechselkurs
dair vek-sel-koors
exchange rate

Do I have...	Muss ich...
	moos ikh
...to key in my PIN?	...meine Geheimzahl eingeben?
	my-ne ge-hime-tsal ine-gay-ben
...to sign here?	...hier unterschreiben?
	heer oon-ter-shry-ben
Is there a cash machine?	Gibt es einen Geldautomaten?
	geept es ine-nen gelt-ow-toe-mah-ten
Can I withdraw money on my credit card?	Kann ich Geld mit meiner Kreditkarte abheben?
	kunn ikh gelt mit my-ner kray-deet-kar-te up-hay-ben
Can I cash a check?	Kann ich einen Scheck einlösen?
	kunn ikh ine-nen shek ine-lur-zen
When does the bank open/close?	Wann öffnet/schließt die Bank?
	vun urf-net/shleest dee bunk

der Geldautomat
dair
gelt-ow-toe-maht
cash machine

die Kreditkarte
dee
kray-deet-kar-te
credit card

das Scheckbuch
dus
shek-bookh
checkbook

STORES

der Fischhändler
dair fish-hendler
fish seller

der Lebensmittelladen
dair lay-bens-mit-tel-lah-den
produce stand

der Gemüseladen
dair ge-mew-ze-lahden
grocery

das Delikatessengeschäft
dus deli-kah-tessen-gesheft
delicatessen

der Bäcker
dair bek-ker
bakery

die Buchhandlung
dee bookh-hundloong
bookstore

der Supermarkt
dair zooper-markt
supermarket

die Fleischerei
dee fly-shuh-rye
butcher

der Tabakladen
dair tah-buk-lah-den
tobacconist

das Möbelgeschäft
dus mur-bel-gesheft
furniture store

der Eisenwarenhändler
dair eye-zen-vahren-hendler
hardware store

die Boutique
dee booteek
boutique

der Schneider
dair shny-der
tailor

der Juwelier
dair yoo-vay-leer
jewelry store

das Schuhgeschäft
dus shoo-gesheft
shoe store

AT THE MARKET

I would like...	Ich hätte gern... *ikh het-te gairn*
How much is this?	Wie viel kostet das? *vee-feel kos-tet dus*
What's the price per kilo?	Wie viel kostet ein Kilo? *vee-feel kos-tet ine kee-lo*
It's too expensive	Das ist zu teuer *dus ist tsoo toy-er*
Do you have anything cheaper?	Haben Sie etwas Billigeres? *hah-ben zee et-vus billy-gair-es*
That's fine, I'll take it	Das ist gut, ich nehme es *dus ist goot ikh nay-me es*
I'll take two kilos	Ich nehme zwei Kilo *ikh nay-me tsvy kee-lo*
A kilo of...	Ein Kilo von... *ine kee-lo fon*
Half a kilo of...	Ein Pfund von... *ine pfoont fon*
A little more, please	Bitte etwas mehr *bit-te et-vus mair*
May I taste it?	Kann ich es kosten? *kunn ikh es kos-ten*
That will be all, thank you	Das ist alles, danke *dus ist alles dun-ke*

YOU MAY HEAR...

Sie wünschen bitte? *zee vewn-shen bit-te* **May I help you?**	Wie viel möchten Sie? *vee-feel murkh-ten zee* **How much would you like?**

IN THE SUPERMARKET

Where is/are...	Wo ist/sind...
	vo ist/zint
...the frozen foods	...die Tiefkühlkost?
	dee teef-kewl-kost
...the beverage aisle?	...der Gang mit den Getränken?
	dair gung mit dain ge-tren-ken
...the checkout?	...die Kasse?
	dee kuss-se
I'm looking for...	Ich suche nach...
	ikh soo-khe nakh

der Einkaufswagen
dair ine-kowfs-vahgen
grocery cart

der Einkaufskorb
dair ine-kowfs-korp
basket

Do you have any more?	Haben Sie noch mehr davon?
	hah-ben zee nokh mair du-fon
Is this reduced?	Ist das reduziert?
	ist dus re-doo-tsiert
Where do I pay?	Wo kann ich zahlen?
	vo kunn ikh tsah-len
Shall I key in my PIN?	Soll ich meine Geheimzahl eingeben?
	zoll ikh my-ne ge-hime-tsal ine-gay-ben
May I have a bag?	Kann ich eine Tüte haben?
	kunn ikh ine-e tew-te hah-ben

FRUIT

die Orange
dee o-run-dsche
orange

die Zitrone
dee tsee-troh-ne
lemon

der Pfirsich
dair pfeehr-zikh
peach

die Nektarine
dee nek-tah-ree-ne
nectarine

die Limone
dee lee-moh-ne
lime

die Kirschen
dee keer-shen
cherries

die Aprikose
dee upri-ko-ze
apricot

die Pflaume
dee pflow-me
plum

die Grapefruit
dee grape-fruit
grapefruit

die Blaubeeren
dee blow-beh-ren
blueberries

die Erdbeere
dee airt-beh-re
strawberry

die Himbeere
dee him-beh-re
raspberry

die Melone
dee may-lo-ne
melon

die Weintrauben
dee vine-trow-ben
grapes

die Banane
dee ba-na-ne
banana

der Granatapfel
dair grah-naht-up-fel
pomegranate

der Apfel
dair up-fel
apple

die Birne
dee beer-ne
pear

die Ananas
dee ana-nahs
pineapple

die Mango
dee mun-go
mango

VEGETABLES

die Kartoffel
dee kar-toffel
potato

die Karotten
dee kah-rotten
carrots

die
Paprikaschote
dee pap-ree-kah-shoh-te
pepper

die
Chillischoten
dee chilli-shoh-ten
chili peppers

die Aubergine
dee oh-bair-gee-ne
eggplant

die Tomate
dee toh-mah-te
tomato

die Zwiebel
dee tsvee-bel
onion

der
Knoblauch
dair khnop-lowkh
garlic

die
Frühlingszwiebel
dee frew-lings-tsvee-bel
scallion

der Lauch
dair lowkh
leek

die Pilze
dee piltse
mushroom

die Zucchini
dee tsoo-kee-nee
zucchini

die Erbsen
dee airp-zen
garden peas

die grüne Bohnen
dee grew-ne boh-nen
green beans

die Gurke
dee goor-ke
cucumber

der Sellerie
dair zell-air-ee
celery

der Spinat
dair shpee-naht
spinach

der Brokkoli
dair bro-ko-lee
broccoli

der Salat
dair Zah-laht
lettuce

der Kohl
dair koal
cabbage

MEAT AND POULTRY

May I...

...have a slice of...?

...have a piece of...?

Kann ich...
kunn ikh

...eine Scheibe...haben?
ine-e shy-be...hah-ben

...ein Stück...haben?
ine shtewk...hah-ben

der Schinken
dair shin-ken
cooked ham

das
Hackfleisch
dus huck-flysh
ground beef

das Steak
dus steak
steak

die Leberwurst
dee lay-ber-voorst
liverwurst

das
Kotelett
dus koht-let
chop

die Zervelatwurst
*dee
tsair-veh-laht-voorst*
cervelat sausage

das Hähnchen
dus hen-khen
chicken

die Ente
dee en-te
duck

FISH AND SHELLFISH

die Seebrasse
dee zay-brass-se
sea bream

der Lachs
dair lahkhs
salmon

die Forelle
dee for-rell-le
trout

der Kabeljau
dair kah-bel-yow
cod

der Seebarsch
dair zay-bursh
sea bass

die Makrele
dee muk-ray-le
mackerel

die Krabbe
dee khrub-be
crab

der Hummer
dair hoom-mer
lobster

die Jakobsmuschel
dee yu-kobs-moo-shel
scallop

die Garnele
dee gahr-nay-le
shrimp

BREAD AND CAKES

das Weißbrot
dus vice-broht
white bread

das Roggenbrot
dus roggen-broht
rye bread

die Laugenstangen
dee low-gen-shtan-gen
salt sticks

das Brötchen
dus broht-khen
bread roll

der Käsekuchen
dair kay-ze-koo-khen
cheesecake

die Sachertorte
dee zakher-tor-te
Sachertorte

der Stollen
dair shtoll-len
stollen

der Guglhupf
dair google-hoopf
Guglhupf

die Schokoladentorte
dee shoko-lah-den-tor-t-e
chocolate cake

die Schwarzwälderkirschtorte
dee shvarts-velder-keersh-tor-te
Black Forest cake

DAIRY PRODUCE

die Vollmilch
dee foll-milkh
whole milk

die Halbfettmilch
dee hulp-fet-milkh
reduced-fat milk

die saure Sahne
dee zow-re zah-ne
sour cream

die Schlagsahne
dee shluk-zah-ne
whipped cream

der Joghurt
dair yog-hurt
yogurt

die Butter
dee boot-ter
butter

der Emmentaler
dair emmen-tah-ler
Emmental

der Greyerzer
dair grey-air-tser
Gruyère

der Ziegenkäse
dair tsee-gen-kay-ze
goat's cheese

die Ziegenmilch
dee tsee-gen-milkh
goat's milk

NEWSPAPERS AND MAGAZINES 🎧

Do you have...	Haben Sie... *hah-ben zee*
...a book of stamps?	...ein Briefmarkenheft? *ine breef-mar-ken-heft*
...airmail stamps?	...Luftpostmarken? *looft-posst-mar-ken*
...a pack of envelopes?	...eine Packung Briefumschläge? *ine-e puk-koong breef-oom-shlay-ge*
...some adhesive tape?	...etwas Klebefilm? *et-vus klay-be-film*

die Ansichtskarte
dee un-zikhts-kar-te
postcard

der Bleistift
dair bly-shtift
pencil

die Briefmarken
dee breef-mar-ken
stamps

der Kugelschreiber
dair koo-gel-shry-ber
pen

YOU MAY HEAR...

Wie alt sind Sie?
vee ahlt zint zee
How old are you?

Haben Sie einen Ausweis?
hah-ben zee ine-nen ows-vice
Do you have ID?

...a pack of cigarettes?

...eine Packung Zigaretten?
ine-e pu-koong tsee-gah-ret-ten

...a box of matches?

...eine Schachtel Streichhölzer?
ine-e shakh-tel shtrike-hurl-tser

das Komikheft
dus komic-heft
comic book

das Feuerzeug
dus foyer-tsoyk
lighter

die Buntstifte
dee boont-shtif-te
colored pencils

der Kaugummi
dair kow-goo-mee
chewing gum

die Süßigkeiten
dee zew-sick-ky-ten
candy

der Tabak
dair tah-buk
tobacco

die Zeitschriften
dee tsyt-shrif-ten
magazines

die Zeitung
dee tsy-toong
newspaper

BUYING CLOTHES AND SHOES

I am looking for...	Ich suche... *ikh zoo-khe*
I am size...	Ich habe Größe... *ikh bin grur-se*
Do you have this...	Haben Sie das... *hah-ben zee dus*
...in my size?	...in meiner Größe? *in my-ner grur-se*
...in small?	...in klein? *in kline*
...in medium?	...in mittlerer Größe? *in mit-ler-er grur-se*
...in large?	...in einer großen Größe? *in ine-er grur-sen grur-se*
...in other colors?	...in anderen Farben? *in un-de-ren far-ben*
May I try this on?	Kann ich das anprobieren? *kunn ikh dus un-pro-bee-ren*
It's...	Es ist... *es ist*
...too big	...zu groß *tsoo grohs*
...too small	...zu klein *tsoo kline*
I need...	Ich brauche... *ikh brow-khe*
...a larger size	...eine größere Größe *ine-e grur-se-re grur-se*
...a smaller size	...eine kleinere Größe *ine-e kline-er-e grur-se*
I'll take this one, please	Ich nehme das, bitte *ikh nay-me dus bit-te*

I take shoe size...	Meine Schuhgröße ist...
	my-ne shoo-grur-se ist

May I...	Kann ich...
	kunn ikh

...try this pair?	...dieses Paar anprobieren?
	dee-zes par un-pro-bee-ren

These are...	Die sind...
	dee zint

...too tight	...zu eng
	tsoo eng

...too big	...zu groß
	tsoo grohs

...too small	...zu klein
	tsoo kline

...uncomfortable	...nicht bequem
	nikht be-kvaym

Is there a bigger/ smaller size?	Haben Sie eine größere/ kleinere Größe?
	hah-ben zee ine grur-se-re/ kline-ne-re grur-se

CLOTHES AND SHOE SIZES GUIDE

Women's clothes sizes	US	4	6	8	10	12	14	16	18
	Europe	34	36	38	40	42	44	46	48

Men's clothes sizes	US	36	38	40	42	44	46	48	50
	Europe	46	48	50	52	54	56	58	60

Shoe sizes	US	5	6	7	8	9	10	11	12	13
	Europe	36	37	38	39	40	42	43	45	46

CLOTHES AND SHOES

das Kleid
dus klite
dress

das Abendkleid
dus ah-bent-klite
evening dress

die Jacke
dee yuk-ke
jacket

der Pullover
dair pull-oh-ver
sweater

die Jeans
dee jeans
jeans

der Rock
dair rock
skirt

die Turnschuhe
dee toorn-shoo-e
sneakers

die Stiefel
dee shtee-fel
boots

die Handtasche
dee hunt-tush-e
handbag

der Gürtel
dair gewr-tel
belt

der Anzug
dair un-tsook
suit

der Mantel
dair mun-tel
coat

das Hemd
dus hemt
shirt

das T-Shirt
dus t-shirt
T-shirt

die Shorts
dee shorts
shorts

die Sandalen
dee zun-dah-len
sandals

die Schnürschuhe
dee shnewr-shoo-e
tie shoes

die Schuhe mit hohem Absatz
dee shoo-e mit hohem up-zuts
high-heeled shoes

die Flipflops
dee flip-flops
flip-flops

die Socken
dee zok-ken
socks

AT THE GIFT SHOP

I'd like to...

Ich möchte gern...
ikh murkh-te gairn

...buy a gift for my mother/father

...ein Geschenk für meine Mutter/meinen Vater kaufen
ine geshenk fewr my-ne moo-ter/my-nen fah-ter kow-fen

...buy a gift for a child

...ein Geschenk für ein Kind kaufen
ine geshenk fewr ine kint kow-fen

Can you recommend something?

Können Sie mir etwas empfehlen?
kur-nen zee mir et-vus em-pfay-len

Do you have a box for it?

Haben Sie einen passenden Karton?
hah-ben zee ine-nen pah-senden kar-tohn

Can you gift-wrap it?

Können Sie es als Geschenk verpacken?
kurn-nen zee es als geshenk fair-puk-ken

das Armband
dus arm-bunt
bracelet

die Uhr
dee oor
watch

die Manschettenknöpfe
dee mun-shetten-knurpfe
cufflinks

die Halskette
dee Huls-ket-te
necklace

das Portemonnaie
dus port-mon-neh
wallet

die Puppe
dee poo-pe
doll

das Kuscheltier
dus koo-shel-teer
stuffed animal

die Pralinen
dee prah-lee-nen
chocolates

Have you anything cheaper?	**Haben Sie etwas Billigeres?** *hah-ben zee et-vus billy-gair-es*
Is there a reduction for cash?	**Gibt es eine Ermäßigung bei Bargeldzahlung?** *geept es ine-e air-mehsee-goong by bar-gelt-tsah-loong*
Is there a guarantee?	**Gibt es eine Garantie?** *geept es ine-e gah-run-tee*

YOU MAY HEAR...

Ist es ein Geschenk?
ist es ine geshenk
Is it for a present?

Soll ich es als Geschenk verpacken?
sohl ikh es als geshenk fair-pukken
Shall I gift-wrap it?

PHOTOGRAPHY

I'd like this film developed

Ich möchte gern diesen Film
entwickeln lassen
*ikh murkh-te gairn dee-zen film
ent-vee-keln luss-sen*

When will it be ready?

Wann ist er fertig?
vun ist air fair-tik

Do you have an express
service?

Haben Sie einen Express-Service?
hah-ben zee ine-nen express-service

Does it cost more?

Kostet das mehr?
kos-tet dus mair

die Digitalkamera
dee dee-ghee-tul-kah-meh-ra
digital camera

die Memory Card
dee memory card
memory card

der Bilderrahmen
dair bil-dair-rah-men
photo frame

das Fotoalbum
dus fo-to-ul-boom
photo album

I'd like the one-hour service

Ich möchte gern den Einstunden-Service
ikh murkh-te gairn dain ine-shtoon-den-service

Can you print from this memory stick?

Können Sie von diesem Memory Stick drucken?
kur-nen zee fon dee-zem memory stick droo-ken

das Objektiv
dus ob-yek-teef
lens

die Kamera
dee kah-meh-ra
camera

die Kameratasche
dee kah-meh-ra-tush-e
camera bag

das Blitzlicht
dus blits-likht
flashlight

YOU MAY HEAR...

Welche Bildgröße möchten Sie?
vel-khe bilt-grur-se murkh-ten zee
What size prints do you want?

Matt oder glänzend?
mutt oh-der glen-tsent
Matte or gloss?

AT THE POST OFFICE

I'd like...

Ich möchte gern...
ikh murkh-te gairn

...to register this letter

...diesen Brief per Einschreiben senden
dee-zen breef pair ine-shry-ben zen-den

...to send this airmail

...diesen Brief per Luftpost senden
dee-zen breef pair looft-posst zen-den

...three stamps, please

...drei Briefmarken, bitte
dry breef-marken bit-te

die
Briefmarken
*dee
breef-mar-ken*
stamps

der Briefumschlag
dair breef-oom-shlahk
envelope

die Luftpost
dee looft-posst
airmail

die Ansichtskarte
dee un-zikhts-kar-te
postcard

YOU MAY HEAR...

Was ist der Inhalt?
vus ist dair in-hult
What are the contents?

Welchen Wert hat er?
vel-khen vairt hut air
What is their value?

| How much is...? | Was kostet...? |
| | *vus kos-tet* |

...a letter to...   ...ein Brief...
ine breef

...a postcard to...   ...eine Ansichtskarte...
ine-e un-zikhts-karte

...the United States   ...in die Vereinigten Staaten
in dee fair-eye-nik-ten shtah-ten

...Great Britain   ... nach Großbritannien
nakh gros-bree-tun-nee-yen

...Canada   ...nach Kanada
nakh kah-nah-dah

...Australia   ...nach Australien
nakh ows-trah-lee-en

May I have a receipt?   Kann ich eine Quittung haben?
kunn ikh ine-e kvit-toong hah-ben

das Paket
dus pa-kayt
package

der Kurier
dair koo-reer
courier

der Briefkasten
dair breef-kuss-ten
mailbox

der Briefträger
dair breef-tray-ger
letter carrier

TELEPHONES

Where is the nearest phone shop?
Wo ist der nächste Telefonladen?
voh ist dair naykh-ste teh-le-fohn-lah-den

Who's speaking?
Mit wem spreche ich?
mit vaim shpre-khe ikh

Hello, this is...
Hallo, hier spricht...
hul-lo heer shprikht

I'd like to speak to...
Ich möchte gern mit... sprechen
ikh murkh-te gairn mit... shpre-khen

das Telefon
dus tay-lay-fohn
phone

smartphone
smartphone
smartphone

der Anrufbeantworter
dair un-roof-bay-unt-vor-tair
answering machine

das Handy
dus han-dee
cell phone

das Münztelefon
dus mewnts-tay-lay-fohn
coin-operated phone

INTERNET

Is there an internet café near here?
Gibt es ein Internetcafé in der Nähe?
geept es ine internet-café in dair nay-he

How much do you charge?
Wie viel verlangen Sie?
vee feel fair-lun-gen zee

Do you have wireless internet?
Haben Sie WLAN?
hah-ben zee veh-lun

Can I check my emails?
Kann ich meine E-Mails checken?
kunn ikh my-ne e-mails tsheck-en

I need to send an email
Ich muss eine E-Mail schicken
ikh moos ine-e e-mail shi-ken

What's your email address?
Wie ist Ihre E-Mail-Adresse?
vee ist ee-re e-mail-ah-dres-se

My email address is...
Meine E-Mail-Adresse ist...
my-ne e-mail-ah-dres-se ist

der Laptop
dair lap-top
laptop

die Tastatur
dee tus-tah-toor
keyboard

die Website
dee web-site
website

die E-Mail
dee e-mail
email

SIGHTSEEING

Most towns have a tourist information office and the staff will advise you on local places to visit as well as city walks and bus tours. Opening hours are usually 9.00am to 6.00pm Monday to Friday and Saturday mornings. Many museums close on Mondays as well as on public holidays, so be sure to check the opening times before visiting.

AT THE TOURIST OFFICE

Where is the tourist information office?	**Wo ist das Fremdenverkehrsbüro?** *vo ist dus frem-den-fer-kairs-bew-ro*
Can you...	**Können Sie...** *kur-nen zee*
...recommend a guided tour?	**...eine Stadtführung empfehlen?** *ine-e shtut-few-rung em-pfay-len*
...recommend an excursion?	**...einen Ausflug empfehlen?** *ine-nen ows-flook em-pfay-len*
Is there a museum or art gallery?	**Gibt es hier ein Museum oder eine Kunstgalerie?** *geept es heer ine moo-zay-oom ohder ine-e koonst-gal-le-ree*
Is it open to the public?	**Ist es für die Öffentlichkeit zugänglich?** *ist es fewr dee ur-fent-likh-kite tsoo-geng-likh*
Is there wheelchair access?	**Gibt es Zugang für Rollstuhlfahrer?** *geept es tsoo-gung fewr roll-shtool-fah-rer*
Does it...	**Ist es...** *ist es*
...close on Sundays?	**...am sonntags geschlossen?** *zon-tahks ge-shlos-sen*
...close on public holidays?	**...an Feiertagen geschlossen?** *un fy-er-tah-gen ge-shlos-sen*
How long does it take to get there?	**Wie lange dauert es bis dorthin?** *vee lun-ge dow-ert es bis dort-hin*
Do you have...	**Haben Sie...** *hah-ben zee*
...a street map	**...einen stadtplan** *ine-nen shtut-plun*

VISITING PLACES

What time...	Um wie viel Uhr... *om vee-feel oor*
...do you open?	...öffnen Sie? *urf-nen zee*
...do you close?	...schließen Sie? *shlee-sen zee*
Two adults, please	Zwei Erwachsene, bitte *tsvy air-vakh-ze-ne bit-te*
A family ticket, please	Eine Familienkarte, bitte *ine-e fah-mee-lee-yen-kar-te bit-te*
How much does it cost?	Was kostet das? *vus kos-tet dus*
Are there reductions for...	Gibt es eine Ermäßigung für... *geept es ine-e er-mess-see-goong fewr*
...children?	...Kinder? *kin-der*
...students?	...Studenten? *shtoo-den-ten*

der Stadtplan
dair shtut-plun
street map

die Eintrittskarte
dee ine-trits-kar-te
entrance ticket

der Zugang für
Rollstuhlfahrer
*dair tsoo-gung fewr
roll-shtool-fah-rer*
wheelchair access

Can I buy a guidebook?	**Kann ich einen Führer kaufen?** *kunn ikh ine-nen few-rer kow-fen*
Is there...	**Gibt es...** *geept es*
...an audio guide?	**...eine Audioführung?** *ine-ne owdeeyo-few-roong*
...a guided tour?	**...eine Führung?** *ine-ne few-roong*
...an elevator?	**...einen Lift?** *ine-nen lift*
...a café?	**...ein Café?** *ine kuf-fay*
...a bus tour?	**...eine Busrundfahrt?** *ine-ne boos-roont-fart*
When is the next tour?	**Wann ist die nächste Führung?** *vun ist dee nekh-ste few-roong*

der Stadtrundfahrtbus
dair shtutt-roont-fart-boos
tour bus

YOU MAY HEAR...

Haben Sie einen Studentenausweis?
hah-ben zee ine-nen shtoo-den-ten-ows-vice
Do you have a student ID?

FINDING YOUR WAY

| Excuse me | Entschuldigen Sie, bitte |
| | *ent-shool-dee-gen zee bit-te* |

| Can you help me? | Können sie mir helfen? |
| | *kur-nen zee mir hel-fen* |

| Is this the way to the museum? | Ist das der Weg zum Museum? |
| | *ist dus dair vayk tsoom moo-zay-oom* |

| How do I get to...? | Wie komme ich...? |
| | *vee kom-me ikh* |

| ...the town center? | ...zum Stadtzentrum? |
| | *tsoom shtut-tsen-troom* |

| ...the station? | ...zum Bahnhof? |
| | *tsoom bahn-hohf* |

| ...the museum? | ...zum Museum? |
| | *tsoom moo-zay-oom* |

| ...the art gallery? | ...zur Kunstgalerie? |
| | *tsoor koonst-gal-le-ree* |

| How long does it take? | Wie lange dauert das? |
| | *vee lun-ge dow-ert dus* |

| Is it far? | Ist es weit? |
| | *ist es vyte* |

| Can you show me on the map? | Können Sie es mir auf der Karte zeigen? |
| | *kur-nen zee es mir owf dair kar-te tsy-gen* |

YOU MAY HEAR...

Es ist nicht weit
es ist nikht vyte
It's not far away

Es ist 10 Minuten zu Fuß
es ist tsayn mi-noo-ten tsoo foos
It takes ten minutes by foot

YOU MAY HEAR...

Wir sind hier
veer zint heer
We are here

In diese Richtung
in dee-ze rikh-toong
This way

Gehen Sie geradeaus...
gay-en zee ge-rah-de-ows
Keep going straight...

In die andere Richtung
in dee un-dair-re rikh-toong
That way

...bis ans Ende der Straße...
bis uns en-de dair shtrah-se
...to the end of the street...

Sie stehen direkt davor
zee shtay-en dee-rekht da-for
It's in front of you

...bis zur Ampel
bis tsoor um-pel
...to the traffic lights

Es ist hinter Ihnen
es ist hin-ter eenen
It's behind you

...bis zum Hauptplatz
bis tsoom howpt-pluts
...to the main square

Es ist Ihnen gegenüber
es ist eenen gay-gen-ewber
It's opposite you

Es ist ausgeschildert
es ist ows-ge-shildert
It's signposted

Es ist neben...
es ist nay-ben
It's next to...

Es ist dort drüben
es ist dort drew-ben
It's over there

Am Museum links abbiegen
um moo-zay-oom links up-bee-gen
Turn left at the museum

Nehmen Sie die erste
(Straße)
*nay-men zee dee airs-te
(shtrah-se)*
Take the first street

An der Ampel rechts
abbiegen
*un dair um-pel rekhts
up-bee-gen*
**Turn right at the traffic
lights**

...links/rechts
links/rekhts
...on the left/right

PLACES TO VISIT

das Rathaus
dus raht-hows
town hall

die Brücke
dee brew-ke
bridge

das Museum
dus moo-zay-oom
museum

die Kunstgalerie
dee koonst-gal-le-ree
art gallery

das Denkmal
dus denk-mahl
monument

die Kirche
dee kir-khe
church

das Dorf
dus dorf
village

der Dom
dair dohm
cathedral

das Schloss
dus shloss
castle

der Leuchtturm
dair loykht-toorm
lighthouse

der Hafen
dair ha-fen
harbor

der Weinberg
dair vine-bairk
vineyard

der Park
dair park
park

die Küste
dee kew-ste
coast

der Wasserfall
dair vus-ser-fahl
waterfall

die Berge
dee bair-ge
mountains

OUTDOOR ACTIVITIES

Where can we...	Wo können wir... *vo kur-nen veer*
...go horseback riding?	...reiten? *ry-ten*
...go fishing?	...angeln? *un-geln*
...go swimming?	...schwimmen? *shvim-men*
...go walking?	...wandern? *vun-dern*
Can we...	Können wir... *kur-nen veer*
...rent equipment?	...eine Ausrüstung mieten? *ine-e ows-rewst-toong mee-ten*
...take lessons?	...Unterricht nehmen? *oon-ter-rikht nay-men*
How much per hour?	Was kostet das pro Stunde? *vus kostet dus pro shtoonde*
I'm a beginner	Ich bin Anfänger/Anfängerin *ikh bin unfenger/unfengerin*
I'm very experienced	Ich bin schon recht erfahren *ikh bin shon rekht air-fah-ren*
Where's the amusement park?	Wo ist der Vergnügungspark? *vo ist dair fair-gnew-goongs-park*
Can the children go on all the rides?	Sind Kinder auf allen Attraktionen erlaubt? *zint kin-der owf allen attrak-tsyoh-nen air-lowpt*
Is there a playground?	Gibt es einen Spielplatz? *geept es ine-nen shpeel-pluts*
Is it safe for children?	Ist er kindersicher? *ist air kin-der-zikher*

der Zoo
dair tsoh
zoo

der Spielplatz
dair shpeel-pluts
playground

das Picknick
dus pick-nick
picnic

der Vergnügungspark
dair fair-gnew-goongs-park
fairground

das Angeln
dus an-geln
fishing

das Reiten
dus ry-ten
horseback riding

der Safaripark
dair safari-park
safari park

der Erlebnispark
dair air-lep-nis-park
amusement park

SPORTS AND LEISURE

Germany and Austria can both offer the traveler a wide
range of cultural events, entertainments, and leisure
activities. They have a strong musical tradition with superb
opera houses and concert halls as well as renowned
musical festivals. There is also a wide range of sports
facilities on offer, from Alpine winter sports and climbing
to hiking and cycling in the Black Forest, and watersports
on the many inland lakes and on the northern Baltic and
North Sea coasts of Germany.

LEISURE TIME

I like...	Ich mag... *ikh mahk*
...art and painting	...Kunst und Malerei *koonst oont mah-ler-rye*
...movies and film	...Filme und Kino *fil-me oont kee-no*
...the theater	...das Theater *dus tay-ah-ter*
...opera	...die Oper *dee oh-per*
I prefer...	Ich mag lieber... *ikh mahk lee-ber*
...reading books	...Bücher lesen *bew-kher lay-zen*
...listening to music	...Musik hören *moo-zeek hur-ren*
...watching sports	...Sportereignisse verfolgen *shport-er-yg-nis-se fer-fol-gen*
...going to concerts	...Konzerte besuchen *kon-tsehrte be-soo-khen*
...dancing	...tanzen gehen *tun-tsen gay-en*
...going to clubs	...in die Disco gehen *in dee disco gay-en*
...going out with friends	...mit Freunden ausgehen *mit froyn-den ows-gay-en*
I don't like...	Ich mag nicht... *ikh mahk nikht*
That doesn't interest me	Das interessiert mich nicht *dus in-ter-es-seert mikh nikht*
That bores me	Das finde ich langweilig *dus fin-de ikh lung-vy-lik*

AT THE BEACH

SPORTS AND LEISURE

Can I...	Kann ich... *kunn ikh*
...rent a jet ski?	...einen Jetski mieten? *ine-nen jetskee mee-ten*
...rent a beach umbrella?	...einen Sonnenschirm mieten? *ine-nen zon-nen-sheerm mee-ten*
...rent a surfboard?	...ein Surfboard leihen? *ine zurf-board ly-en*

das Strandlaken
dus shtrunt-lah-ken
beach towel

der Liegestuhl
dair lee-ge-shtool
deck chair

der Wasserball
dair vus-ser-bahl
beach ball

die Sonnenliege
dee zon-nen-lee-ge
lounge chair

YOU MAY HEAR...

Schwimmen verboten
shvim-men fair-bo-ten
No swimming

Der Strand ist gesperrt
dair shtrant ist ge-shpairt
Beach closed

Starke Strömung
shtar-ke shtrur-moong
Strong currents

123 AT THE BEACH

How much does it cost?	Was kostet das?
	vus kos-tet dus
Can I go water-skiing?	Kann ich Wasserski fahren?
	kunn ikh vus-ser-shee fah-ren
Is there a lifeguard?	Ist ein Rettungsschwimmer da?
	ist ine ret-toongs-shvim-mer dah
Is it safe to...	Kann man...
	kunn mun
...swim here?	...hier schwimmen?
	heer shvim-men
...surf here?	...hier surfen?
	heer zur-fen

die Sonnenbrille
dee zon-nen-bril-le
sunglasses

der Sonnenhut
dair zon-nen-hoot
sun hat

die Schwimmflossen
dee shvim-flos-sen
fins

das Sonnenschutzmittel
dus zon-nen-shoots-mittel
suntan lotion

der Bikini
dair bee-kee-nee
bikini

die Maske/der
Schnorchel
*dee mas-ke/dair
shnor-khel*
mask/snorkel

AT THE SWIMMING POOL

What time...	Um wie viel Uhr... *oom vee-feel oor*
...does the pool open?	...öffnet das Schwimmbad? *urf-net dus shvim-baht*
...does the pool close?	...schließt das Schwimmbad? *shleest dus shvim-baht*
Is it...	Ist es... *ist es*
...an indoor pool?	...ein Hallenbad? *ine hull-en-baht*
...an outdoor pool?	...ein Freibad? *ine fry-baht*
Is there a children's pool?	Gibt es ein Kinderbecken? *geept es ine kin-der-bek-ken*
Where are the changing rooms?	Wo sind die Umkleidekabinen? *vo zint dee oom-kly-de-kah-beenen*

die
Schwimmflügel
*dee
shvim-flew-gel*
water wings

die
Schwimmbretter
dee shvimm-bret-ter
floats

die Schwimmbrille
dee shvim-brill-le
swimming goggles

der Badeanzug
dair bah-de-un-tsook
swimsuit

AT THE GYM

der Crosstrainer
dair cross-trainer
cross trainer

das Trainingsrad
dus trai-nings-raht
exercise bike

die Rudermaschine
dee roo-der-mah-shee-ne
rowing machine

der Stepper
dair step-per
step machine

Is there a gym?	Gibt es hier ein Fitnessstudio? *geept es heer ine fit-ness-shtoo-dee-yoh*
Is it free for guests?	Ist es für Gäste kostenlos? *ist es fewr ges-te kos-ten-los*
Do I have to wear sneakers?	Muss ich Turnschuhe tragen? *moos ikh toorn-shoo-e trah-gen*
Do I need an introductory session?	Muss ich an einer Einführung teilnehmen? *moos ikh un ine-er ine-few-roong tile-nay-men*
Do you hold...	Haben Sie... *hah-ben zee*
...aerobics classes?	...Aerobic-Kurse? *aerobic-koor-ze*
...Pilates classes?	...Pilates-Kurse? *pee-la-tes-koor-ze*
...yoga classes?	...Yoga-Kurse? *yoga-koor-ze*

BOATING AND SAILING

Can I...	Kann ich... _kunn ikh_
...rent a dinghy?	...ein Schlauchboot mieten? _ine shlowkh-boht mee-ten_
...rent a windsurfer?	...einen Windsurfer mieten? _ine-nen vint-zur-fer mee-ten_
...rent a canoe?	...ein Kanu mieten? _ine kah-noo mee-ten_
...rent a rowboat?	...ein Ruderboot mieten? _ine roo-der-boht mee-ten_
Do you offer sailing lessons?	Geben Sie Segelunterricht? _gay-ben zee zay-gel-oon-ter-rikht_
Do you have a mooring?	Haben Sie einen Liegeplatz? _hah-ben zee ine-nen lee-ge-pluts_
How much is it for the night?	Wie viel kostet es pro Nacht? _vee-feel kos-tet es pro nakht_
Where can I buy gas?	Wo kann ich Gas kaufen? _vo kunn ikh gus kow-fen_
Where is the marina?	Wo ist der Jachthafen? _vo ist dair yakht-hah-fen_
Are there life jackets?	Sind Schwimmwesten vorhanden? _zint shvim-ves-ten for-han-den_

die
Schwimmweste
dee shvim-ves-te
life jacket

der Kompass
dair kom-pus
compass

WINTER SPORTS

I would like to...	Ich möchte gern... *ikh murkh-te gairn*
...rent some skis	...Skier leihen *shee-er ly-hen*
...rent some ski boots	...Skistiefel leihen *shee-shtee-fel ly-hen*
...rent some poles	...Skistöcke leihen *shee-shtur-ke ly-hen*
...rent a snowboard	...ein Snowboard leihen *ine snow-board ly-hen*
...rent a helmet	...einen Sturzhelm leihen *ine-nen shtoorts-helm ly-hen*
When does...	Wann... *vun*
...the chair lift start?	...fährt der erste Sessellift? *fairt dair airs-te zes-sel-lift*
...the cable car finish?	...fährt die letzte Seilbahn? *fairt dee lets-te zile-bahn*
How much is a lift pass?	Was kostet ein Liftpass? *vus kos-tet ine lift-pass*
Can I take skiing lessons?	Kann ich Skiunterricht nehmen? *kunn ikh shee-oon-ter-rikht nay-men*
Where are the green slopes?	Wo sind die Anfängerhügel? *vo zint dee un-fenger-hew-gel*

YOU MAY HEAR...

Sind Sie Anfänger/Anfängerin? *zind zee un-fenger/un-fenger-in* **Are you a beginner?**	Ich brauche eine Kaution *ikh brow-khe ine-e kow-tsee-yon* **I need a deposit**

BALL GAMES

I like playing...	Ich spiele gern... *ikh shpee-le gairn*
...soccer	...Fußball *foos-bahl*
...tennis	...Tennis *tennis*
...golf	...Golf *golf*
...badminton	...Badminton *badminton*
...squash	...Squash *skwosh*
...baseball	...Baseball *baseball*
Where is the nearest...	Wo ist der nächste... *vo ist dair nekh-ste*
...tennis court?	...Tennisplatz? *tennis-pluts*
...golf course?	...Golfplatz? *golf-pluts*

der Fußball
dair foos-bahl
soccer ball

der Korb
dair korp
basket

der Baseballhandschuh
dair base-ball-hunt-shoo
baseball glove

May I...	Kann ich... *kunn ikh*
...book a court for two hours?	...einen Platz für zwei Stunden buchen? *ine-nen pluts fewr tsvy shtoon-den boo-khen*
...book a court at three o'clock?	...einen Platz für drei Uhr buchen? *ine-nen pluts fewr dry oor boo-khen*
What shoes are allowed?	Welche Schuhe sind erlaubt? *vel-khe shoo-he zint air-lowpt*
Can I...	Kann ich... *kunn ikh*
...rent a tennis racquet?	...einen Tennisschläger mieten? *ine-nen tennis-shlay-ger mee-ten*
...rent some balls?	...einige Bälle mieten? *ine-ige bell-le mee-ten*
...rent a set of clubs?	...ein Golfset mieten? *ine golf-set mee-ten*

der Golfschläger
dair golf-shlay-ger
golf club

die Tennisbälle
dee tennis-bell-le
tennis balls

der Golfball und
das Golf-Tee
*dair golf-bahl
oont dus golf-tee*
golf ball and tee

die Schweißbänder
dee shvyss-ben-der
sweatbands

der Tennisschläger
dair tennis-shlay-ger
tennis racket

GOING OUT

Where is...	Wo ist... *vo ist*
...the opera house?	...die Oper? *dee oh-pair*
...a jazz club?	...ein Jazzclub? *ine jazz-kloob*
Do I have to book in advance?	Muss ich vorab buchen? *moos ikh for-up boo-khen*
I'd like...tickets	Ich möchte...Karten *ikh murkh-te...kar-ten*
I'd like seats...	Ich möchte Sitze... *ikh murkh-te zit-se*
...at the back	...hinten *hin-ten*
...at the front	...vorne *for-ne*
...in the middle	...in der Mitte *in dair mi-te*
...in the balcony	...auf dem Rang *owf daim rung*
Can I buy a program?	Kann ich ein Programm kaufen? *kunn ikh ine pro-gramm kow-fen*
Is there live music?	Wird live gespielt? *veert live ge-shpeelt*

YOU MAY HEAR...

Schalten Sie Ihr
Handy aus
*shulten zee eer
handy ows*
Turn off your cell phone

Kehren Sie zu Ihren
Plätzen zurück
*kair-ren zee tsoo ee-ren
plet-sen tsoo-rewk*
Return to your seats

der Musiker
dair moo-zee-ker
musician

das Theater
dus tay-ah-ter
theater

das Opernhaus
dus oh-pairn-hows
opera house

der Nachtclub
dair nakht-kloob
nightclub

der Pianist
dair pee-ah-nist
pianist

der Sänger/die
Sängerin
dair zen-ger/dee
zen-gerin
singer

das Kino
dus kee-no
movie theater

das Popcorn
dus pop-corn
popcorn

das Ballett
dus bah-let
ballet

das Kasino
dus kah-zee-no
casino

GALLERIES AND MUSEUMS 🎧

What are the opening hours?	Was sind die Öffnungszeiten? *vus zint dee urf-noongs-tsy-ten*
Are there guided tours in English?	Gibt es Führungen auf Englisch? *geept es few-run-gen owf eng-lish*
When does the tour leave?	Wann beginnt die Besichtigungstour? *vun beginnt dee be-zikh-tee-goongs-toor*
How much does it cost?	Wie viel kostet es? *vee-feel kos-tet es*
How long does it take?	Wie lange dauert es? *vee lun-ghe dowert es*
Do you have an audio guide?	Haben Sie eine Audioführung? *hah-ben zee ine-ne ow-dee-oh-few-roong*
Do you have a guidebook in English?	Haben Sie einen Führer auf Englisch? *hah-ben zee ine-nen few-rer owf eng-lish*
Is (flash) photography allowed?	Ist das Fotografieren (mit Blitzlicht) erlaubt? *ist dus fo-to-gra-fee-ren (mit blits-likht) air-lowpt*

die Statue
dee shta-too-e
statue

die Büste
dee bews-te
bust

Can you direct me to...?	Wie finde ich...? *vee fin-de ikh*
I'd really like to see the pictures	Ich möchte gern die Bilder sehen *ikh murkh-te gairn dee bil-der zay-en*
Who painted this?	Wer hat das gemalt? *vair hut dus ge-mahlt*
How old is it?	Wie alt ist es? *vee ult ist es*
Are there wheelchair ramps?	Gibt es Rollstuhlrampen? *geept es roll-shtool-rum-pen*
Is there an elevator?	Ist ein Lift da? *ist ine lift dah*
Where are the restrooms?	Wo sind die Toiletten? *vo zint dee twah-let-ten*
I've lost my group	Ich habe meine Gruppe verloren *ikh hah-be my-ne groo-pe fair-lo-ren*

das Gemälde
dus ge-mel-de
painting

die Zeichnung
dee tsykh-noong
drawing

der Stich
dair shtikh
engraving

das Manuskript
dus mah-noos-kript
manuscript

HOME ENTERTAINMENT

How do I...	Wie... *vee*
...turn on the television?	...stelle ich den Fernseher an? *shtelle ikh dain fairnzayer un*
...change channels?	...wechsle ich die Kanäle? *vekhs-le ikh dee kahnayle*
...turn up the volume?	...stelle ich den Ton lauter? *shtel-le ikh dain tohn lowtair*
...turn down the volume?	...stelle ich den Ton leiser? *shtel-le ikh den tohn lyzair*
Do you have satellite TV?	Haben Sie Satelliten-Fernsehen? *hah-ben zee za-tel-lee-ten-fairnzayen*
Where can I...	Wo kann ich... *vo kunn ikh*
...buy a DVD?	...eine DVD kaufen? *ine-e deh fow deh kow-fen*
...buy a music CD?	...eine Musik-CD kaufen? *ine-e moozik-tseh-deh kow-fen*

der Breitbild-Fernseher
dair brite-bilt-fairnzayer
widescreen TV

der DVD-Player
dair deh fow deh player
DVD player

die Fernbedienung
dee fairn-be-dee-nung
remote control

das Videospiel
dus vee-de-oh-shpeel
video game

USB-Stick
oo es beh stick
USB flash drive

der Laptop
dair lap-top
laptop

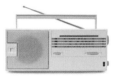

das Radio
dus rah-dee-oh
radio

Festplatte
fest-plut-te
hard drive

die Maus
dee mows
mouse

Can I use this to...	Kann ich damit... *kunn ikh dah-mit*
...go online?	...online gehen? *on-line gay-en*
Is it broadband/wifi?	Ist es ein Breitband-/WLAN-Anschluss? *ist es ine brite-bant/veh-lun-un-shloos*
How do...	Wie... *Vee*
...I log on?	...logge ich mich ein? *log-ge ikh mikh ine*
...I log out?	...logge ich mich aus? *log-ge ikh mikh ows*

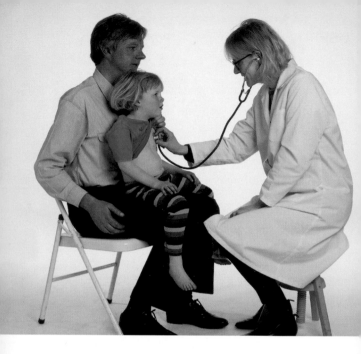

HEALTH

EU nationals receive free emergency medical care in Germany and Austria, provided they produce a European Health Insurance Card. Visitors from other countries should check that their health insurance covers them for medical treatment abroad, or purchase special travel insurance. It is a good idea to familiarize yourself with a few basic phrases in case you need to visit a pharmacy or doctor.

USEFUL PHRASES

I need a doctor	Ich brauche einen Arzt *ikh brow-khe ine-nen artst*
I would like...	Ich hätte gerne... *ikh het-te gair-ne*
...an appointment today	...heute einen Termin *hoy-te ine-nen tair-min*
...an appointment tomorrow	...morgen einen Termin *mor-gen ine-nen tair-min*
It's very urgent	Es ist sehr dringend *es ist zair drin-gent*
I have a European Health Insurance Card	Ich habe eine Europäische Krankenversicherungskarte *ikh hah-be ine-e oyro-pay-ee-shuh krunk-en-fair-zikher-oongs-kar-te*
I have health insurance	Ich habe eine Krankenversicherung *ikh hah-be ine-e krunk-en-fair-zikher-oong*
May I have a receipt?	Kann ich eine Quittung haben? *kunn ikh ine-ne kvit-toong hah-ben*
Where is...	Wo ist... *vo ist*
...the nearest pharmacy?	...die nächste Apotheke? *dee nekh-ste apo-tay-ke*
...the nearest doctor's office?	...die nächste Arztpraxis? *dee nekh-ste artst-pra-xis*
...the nearest hospital?	...das nächste Krankenhaus? *dus nekh-ste krunken-hows*
...the nearest dentist?	...der nächste Zahnarzt? *dair nekh-ste tsahn-artst*

AT THE PHARMACY

What can I take for...?	Was hilft gegen...? *vus hilft gay-gen*
How many should I take?	Wie viele soll ich davon nehmen? *vee-feel-e zoll ikh dah-fon nay-men*
Is it safe for children?	Ist es für Kinder ungefährlich? *ist es fewr kin-der oon-ge-fair-likh*
Are there side effects?	Gibt es Nebenwirkungen? *geept es nayben-veer-koon-gen*
Do you have that...	Haben Sie das... *hah-ben zee dus*
...in tablet form?	...als Tabletten? *uls tub-let-ten*
...as a spray	...als Spray? *uls spray*
...in capsule form?	...in Kapselform? *in kup-sel-form*
I'm allergic to...	Ich bin allergisch gegen... *ikh bin ul-lair-gish gay-gen*
I'm already taking...	Ich nehme bereits... *ikh nay-me be-rites*
Do I need a prescription?	Brauche ich ein Rezept? *brow-khe ikh ine ray-tsept*

YOU MAY HEAR...

Sie nehmen das...mal am Tag
zee nay-men dus...mul um tahk
Take this...times a day

Während der Mahlzeiten *vairent dair mahl-tsyten* **With food**	Vor den Mahlzeiten *for dain mahl-tsyten* **Before eating**

die Bandage
dee bun-dah-she
bandage

das Pflaster
dus pflus-ter
adhesive bandage

die Kapsel
dee kup-sel
capsule

die Tablette
dee tub-let-te
pill

die Salbe
dee zul-be
ointment

das Zäpfchen
dus tsepf-khen
suppository

die Tropfen
dee tropf-en
drops

der Inhalator
dair in-ha-la-tor
inhaler

das Spray
dus shpray
spray

der Sirup
dair zee-roop
syrup

THE HUMAN BODY

I have hurt my knee Ich habe mir das Knie verletzt
ikh hah-be meer dus k-nee fair-letst

der Ellbogen
dair el-bo-gen
elbow

der Arm
dair arm
arm

der Kopf
dair kopf
head

die Schulter
dee shool-ter
shoulder

der Nacken
dair nak-ken
neck

die Brust
dee broost
chest

der Bauch
dair bowkh
stomach

das Bein
dus bine
leg

das Knie
dus k-nee
knee

der Fuß
dair foos
foot

FACE

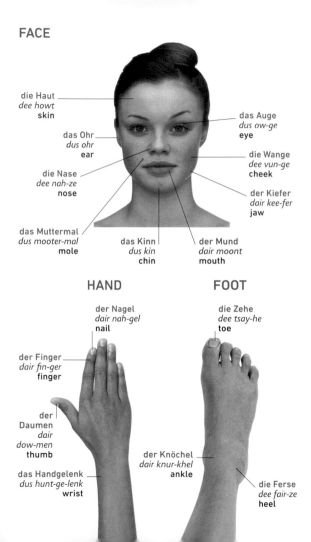

die Haut
dee howt
skin

das Auge
dus ow-ge
eye

das Ohr
dus ohr
ear

die Wange
dee vun-ge
cheek

die Nase
dee nah-ze
nose

der Kiefer
dair kee-fer
jaw

das Muttermal
dus mooter-mal
mole

das Kinn
dus kin
chin

der Mund
dair moont
mouth

HAND

FOOT

der Nagel
dair nah-gel
nail

die Zehe
dee tsay-he
toe

der Finger
dair fin-ger
finger

der
Daumen
*dair
dow-men*
thumb

der Knöchel
dair knur-khel
ankle

das Handgelenk
dus hunt-ge-lenk
wrist

die Ferse
dee fair-ze
heel

FEELING SICK

I don't feel well	Ich fühle mich nicht wohl *ikh few-le mikh nikht vohl*
I feel sick	Ich bin krank *ikh bin krunk*
I have...	Ich habe... *ikh hah-be*
...an ear ache	...Ohrenschmerzen *oh-ren-shmairt-sen*
...a stomach ache	...Bauchschmerzen *bowkh-shmairt-sen*
...a sore throat	...Halsschmerzen *huls-shmairt-sen*
...a temperature	...Fieber *fee-ber*
...hayfever	...Heuschnupfen *hoy-shnoop-fen*
...constipation	...Verstopfung *fair-shtopf-oong*
...diarrhea	...Durchfall *doorkh-full*
...toothache	...Zahnschmerzen *tsahn-shmairt-sen*
I've been...	Mich hat... *mikh hut*
...stung by a bee/wasp	...eine Biene/Wespe gestochen *ine-e bee-ne/ves-pe ge-shto-khen*
...stung by a jellyfish	...eine Qualle gestochen *ine-e kval-le ge-shto-khen*
...bitten by a dog	...ein Hund gebissen *ine hoont ge-bis-sen*

INJURIES

die Bisswunde
dee bis-voon-de
bite

die Stichwunde
dee shtikh-voon-de
sting

der Bruch
dair brookh
fracture

die Schramme
dee shrum-me
graze

der Splitter
dair shplit-ter
splinter

die Brandwunde
dee brunt-voon-de
burn

die Schnittwunde
dee shnit-voon-de
cut

die Prellung
dee prel-loong
bruise

der Sonnenbrand
dair zon-nen-brunt
sunburn

die Verstauchung
dee fair-shtow-khung
sprain

AT THE DOCTOR

I'm...	Ich... *ikh*
...vomiting	...muss mich erbrechen *moos mikh air-brekhen*
...bleeding	...blute *bloo-te*
I'm feeling dizzy	Mir ist schwindlig *meer ist shvind-lik*
I'm feeling faint	Ich fühle mich schwach *ikh few-le mikh shvakh*
I'm pregnant	Ich bin schwanger *ikh bin shvun-ger*
I'm diabetic	Ich bin Diabetiker/Diabetikerin *ikh bin dee-ar-bay-ti-kair/* *dee-ar-bay-ti-kair-in*
I'm epileptic	Ich bin Epileptiker/ Epileptikerin *ikh bin eh-pee-lep-ti-kair/* *eh-pee-lep-ti-kair-in*
I have arthritis	Ich habe Arthritis *ikh hah-be ar-tree-tis*
I have a heart condition	Ich bin herzkrank *ikh bin hairts-krunk*
I have high blood pressure	Ich habe hohen Blutdruck *ikh hah-be ho-hen* *bloot-drook*

YOU MAY HEAR...

Was fehlt Ihnen?
vus failt ee-nen
What's wrong?

Wo tut es weh?
vo toot es vay
Where does it hurt?

ILLNESS

die Erkältung
dee air-kel-tung
cold

der Husten
dair hoos-ten
cough

die Grippe
dee grip-pe
the flu

das Asthma
dus asth-mah
asthma

das Nießen
dus nee-sen
sneeze

die Krämpfe
dee krem-fe
cramps

die Übelkeit
dee ew-bel-kite
nausea

der Ausschlag
dair ows-shlahk
rash

das Nasenbluten
dus nah-zen-bloo-ten
nosebleed

die Kopfschmerzen
dee kopf-shmairt-sen
headache

AT THE HOSPITAL

Can you help me?	**Können Sie mir helfen?** *kurn-nen zee mir hel-fen*
I need...	**Ich brauche...** *ikh brow-ke*
...a doctor	**...einen Arzt** *ine-nen artst*
...a nurse	**...eine Krankenschwester** *ine-e krun-ken-shves-ter*
Where is...	**Wo ist...** *vo ist*
...the emergency room?	**...die Unfallstation?** *dee oon-full-shta-tsee-yon*
...the children's ward?	**...die Kinderstation?** *dee kin-der-shtah-tsee-yon*
...the X-ray department?	**...die Röntgenabteilung?** *dee rurnt-gen-up-ty-loong*
...the waiting room?	**...das Wartezimmer?** *dus var-te-tsim-mer*

die Injektion
dee in-yek-tsee-yon
injection

das Röntgenbild
dus rurnt-gen-bilt
X-ray

die Blutprobe
dee bloot-proh-be
blood test

der Ultraschall
dair ool-tra-shul
scan

...the intensive care unit?   ...die Intensivstation?
                               dee in-tenseev-shta-tsee-yon

...the elevator/stairs?   ...der Lift/die Treppe?
                               dair Lift/dee trep-pe

I think I've broken   Ich glaube, ich habe mir den
my arm   Arm gebrochen
                               ikh glow-be ikh hah-be mir
                               dain arm ge-brokhen

Do I need...   Brauche ich...
                               brow-khe ikh

...an injection?   ...eine Injektion?
                               ine-e in-yek-tsee-yon

...antibiotics?   ...Antibiotika?
                               anti-bee-oh-tee-kah

...an operation?   ...eine Operation?
                               ine-e o-pay-rah-tsee-yon

Will it hurt?   Tut das weh?
                               toot dus vay

How long will it take?   Wie lange wird es dauern?
                               vee lun-ge virt es dow-ern

die Wiederbelebung
dee vee-der-be-lay-boong
resuscitation

der Rollstuhl
dair roll-shtool
wheelchair

die Schiene
dee shee-ne
splint

der Verband
dair fair-bunt
dressing

EMERGENCIES

In you are involved in an accident in Germany, you must dial 110 for the police (*Polizei*), whether or not there are injuries. Use 112 to call an ambulance (*Krankenwagen*) or the fire department (*Feurwehr*). If you are the victim of a crime or you lose your passport and money or other possessions, you should report the incident to the police without delay.

IN AN EMERGENCY

Help!	**Hilfe!** *hil-fe*
Please go away!	**Gehen Sie bitte!** *gay-en zee bit-te*
Let go!	**Loslassen!** *lohs-las-sen*
Stop! Thief!	**Halt! Diebstahl!** *hult deep-shtahl*
Call the police!	**Rufen Sie die Polizei!** *roo-fen zee dee po-lit-sye*
Get a doctor!	**Holen Sie einen Arzt!** *ho-len zee ine-nen artst*
I need...	**Ich brauche...** *ikh brow-khe*
...the police	**...die Polizei** *dee po-lit-sye*
...the fire department	**...die Feuerwehr** *dee foyer-vair*
...an ambulance	**...einen Krankenwagen** *ine-nen krun-ken-vah-gen*
It's very urgent	**Es ist dringend** *es ist drin-gent*
Where is...	**Wo ist...** *vo ist*
...the American/British embassy?	**...die amerikanische/Britische Botschaft?** *dee amerikahnishe/bri-tishe boht-shaft*
...the American/British consulate?	**...das amerikanische/Britische Konsulat?** *dus amerikahnishe/bri-tishe kon-zoo-lut*
...the police station?	**...die Polizeiwache?** *dee po-lit-sye-vakhe*
...the hospital?	**...das Krankenhaus?** *dus krun-ken-hows*

ACCIDENTS

I need to make a telephone call	Ich muss telefonieren *ikh moos tay-lay-fo-nee-ren*
I'd like to report an accident	Ich möchte einen Unfall melden *ikh murkh-te ine-nen oon-fal mel-den*
I've crashed my car	Ich habe einen Autounfall gehabt *ikh hah-be ine-nen ow-toe oon-fall e-hupt*
The registration number is...	Das amtliche Kennzeichen ist... *dus amt-likh-e ken-tsye-khen ist*
I'm at...	Ich befinde mich... *ikh be-fin-de mikh*
Please come quickly!	Kommen Sie bitte schnell! *kom-men zee bit-te shnel*
Someone's injured	Jemand ist verletzt *yay-munt ist fair-letst*
Someone's been knocked down	Jemand ist überfahren worden *yay-munt ist ew-ber-fah-ren vor-den*
There's a fire at my home	Bei mir ist ein Feuer ausgebrochen *by mir ist ine foy-er ows-ge-brokhen*

YOU MAY HEAR...

Welchen Notdienst brauchen Sie?
vel-khen noht-deenst brow-khen zee
Which service do you require?

Was ist passiert?
vus ist pah-seert
What happened?

EMERGENCY SERVICES

der Hydrant
dair hew-drant
hydrant

die Feuerwehrleute
dee foyer-vair-loy-te
firefighters

der Feuerlöscher
dair foyer-lur-sher
fire extinguisher

das Polizeiauto
dus po-lit-sye-ow-toe
police car

die Handschellen
dee hunt-shel-len
handcuffs

der Feueralarm
dair foyer-ah-larm
fire alarm

der Krankenwagen
dair krun-ken-vah-gen
ambulance

der Polizist
dair po-lit-sist
police officer

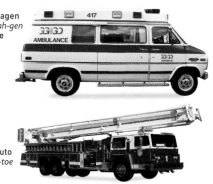

das Feuerwehrauto
dus foyer-vair-ow-toe
fire engine

EMERGENCIES

POLICE AND CRIME

I want to report a crime	**Ich möchte ein Verbrechen melden** *ikh murkh-te ine fer-brekh-en mel-den*
I've been...	**Ich bin...** *ikh bin*
...robbed	**...bestohlen worden** *be-shtoh-len vor-den*
...mugged	**...Opfer eines Straßenraubs geworden** *op-fer ine-es shtra-sen-rowps ge-vor-den*
...raped	**...vergewaltigt worden** *fair-ge-vul-tigt vor-den*
I've been burgled	**Bei mir ist eingebrochen worden** *by mir ist ine-ge-brokhen vor-den*
Someone has...	**Jemand hat...** *yay-munt hut*
...stolen my car	**...mein Auto gestohlen** *mine ow-toe ge-shtoh-len*
...stolen my money	**...mein Geld gestohlen** *mine gelt ge-shtoh-len*
...stolen my passport	**...meinen Pass gestohlen** *min-en pahs ge-shtoh-len*

YOU MAY HEAR...

Wann ist es passiert?
vun ist es pah-seert
When did it happen?

Wie sah er aus?
vee zah air ows
What did he look like?

Gibt es einen Zeugen?
geept es ine-nen tsoy-gen
Was there a witness?

I'd like to...	Ich möchte... *ikh murkh-te*
...speak to a senior officer	...mit einem leitenden Beamten sprechen *mit ine-nem ly-ten-den bay-um-ten shpray-khen*
...speak to a policewoman	...mit einer Polizeibeamtin sprechen *mit ine-er poh-lee-tsy-be-um-tin shpray-khen*
I need...	Ich brauche... *ikh brow-khe*
...an interpreter	...einen Dolmetscher *ine-nen dol-met-sher*
...to make a phone call	Ich muss telefonieren *ikh moos tay-lay-fo-nee-ren*
I'm very sorry, officer	Das tut mir leid, Herr Offizier *dus toot mir lite herr off-fee-tseer*
Here is...	Hier ist... *heer ist*
...my driver's license	...mein Führerschein *mine few-rer-shine*
...my insurance	...meine Versicherung *my-ne fair-zikh-eroong*

YOU MAY HEAR...

Ihren Führerschein, bitte
ee-ren few-rer-shine bit-te
Your license, please

Ihre Zulassungsnummer?
ee-re tsoo-las-sungs-noo-mer
Your registration number?

AT THE GARAGE

Where is the nearest garage?	**Wo ist die nächste Werkstatt?** *vo ist dee nekh-ste vairk-stut*
Can you do repairs?	**Machen Sie Reparaturen?** *makh-en zee re-pah-ra-tooren*
I need...	**Ich brauche...** *ikh brow-khe*
...a new tire	**...einen neuen Reifen** *ine-nen noy-en rye-fen*
...a new exhaust	**...einen neuen Auspuff** *ine-nen noy-en ows-poof*
...a new windshield	**...eine neue Windschutzscheibe** *ine-e noy-e vint-shoots-shy-be*
...a new headlight	**...eine neue Glühbirne** *ine-e noy-e glew-beer-ne*
...new wiper blades	**...neue Wischerblätter** *noy-e visher-blet-ter*
Do you have one in stock?	**Haben Sie einen/eine/eins auf Lager?** *hah-ben zee ine-nen/ine-ne/ines owf lah-ger*
Can you replace this?	**Können Sie das austauschen?** *kur-nen zee dus ows-tow-shen*
The...is not working	**Der/die/das...funktioniert nicht** *dair/dee/dus foonk-tsee-yoneert nikht*
Is it serious?	**Ist es etwas Ernsthaftes?** *ist es et-vus airnst-huf-tes*
How long will it take?	**Wie lange wird es dauern?** *vee lun-ge veert es dow-ern*
When will it be ready?	**Wann wird es fertig sein?** *vun veert es fer-tik zine*
How much will it cost?	**Wie teuer wird es?** *vee toy-er veert es*

CAR BREAKDOWN

My car has broken down	**Mein Auto hat eine Panne** *mine ow-toe hut ine-e pun-e*
Please can you help me?	**Können Sie mir helfen?** *kur-nen zee mir hel-fen*
Please come to...	**Bitte kommen Sie zu...** *bit-te kom-men zee tsoo*
I have a flat tire	**Ich habe einen Platten** *ikh hah-be ine-nen plut-ten*
Can you help change the wheel?	**Können Sie mir beim Reifenwechsel helfen?** *kur-nen zee mir bym rye-fen-vek-sel hel-fen*
I need a new tire	**Ich brauche einen neuen Reifen** *ikh brow-khe ine-nen noy-en rye-fen*
My car won't start	**Mein Wagen springt nicht an** *mine vah-gen shpringt nikht un*
The engine is overheating	**Der Motor wird zu heiß** *dair mo-tor veert tsoo hice*
Can you fix it?	**Können Sie das reparieren?** *kur-nen zee dus re-pah-reer-en*
I've run out of gas	**Mir ist das Benzin ausgegangen** *mir ist dus ben-tseen ows-ge-gun-gen*

YOU MAY HEAR...

Brauchen Sie Hilfe?
brow-khen zee hil-fe
Do you need any help?

Wo liegt denn das Problem?
vo leegt den dus prob-laym
What is the problem?

LOST PROPERTY

I've...	Ich habe... *ikh hah-be*
...lost my money	...mein Geld verloren *mine gelt fair-lo-ren*
...lost my keys	...meine Schlüssel verloren *my-ne shlews-sel fair-lo-ren*
...lost my glasses	...meine Brille verloren *my-ne bril-le fair-lo-ren*
My luggage is missing	Mein Gepäck ist verloren gegangen *mine ge-pek ist fair-lo-ren ge-gun-gen*
Has it turned up yet?	Ist es schon aufgetaucht? *ist es shon owf-ge-towkht*

die Brieftasche
dee breef-tash-e
wallet

der Pass
dair pahs
passport

die Kreditkarte
dee kray-deet-kar-te
credit card

die Geldbörse
dee gelt-bur-se
change purse

die Kamera
dee ka-me-ra
camera

smartphone
smartphone
smartphone

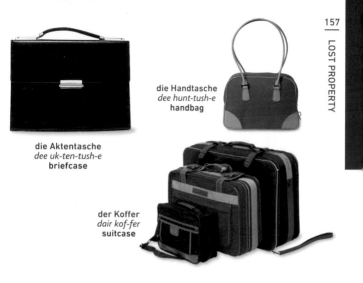

die Handtasche
dee hunt-tush-e
handbag

die Aktentasche
dee uk-ten-tush-e
briefcase

der Koffer
dair kof-fer
suitcase

I need to phone my insurance company	**Ich muss meine Versicherung anrufen** *ikh moos my-ne fair-zikh-air-oong un-roof-en*
Can I put a stop on my credit cards?	**Kann ich meine Kreditkarten sperren?** *kunn ikh my-ne kray-deet-kar-ten shpair-ren*
My name is...	**Mein Name ist...** *mine nah-me ist*
My policy number is...	**Meine Versicherungsnummer ist...** *my-ne fair-zikh-air-oongs -noo-mer ist*
My address is...	**Meine Adresse ist...** *my-ne ad-res-se ist*
My contact number is...	**Meine Telefonnummer ist...** *my-ne tay-lay-fohn-noo-mer ist*
My email address is...	**Meine E-Mail-Adresse ist...** *my-ne email-adres-se ist*

MENU GUIDE

This guide lists the most common terms you may encounter on German menus or when shopping for food. If you can't find an exact phrase, try looking up its component parts.

A

Aal *eel*
am Spieß *on the spit*
Ananas *pineapple*
Äpfel *apples*
Apfel im Schlafrock *baked apple in puff pastry*
Apfelsaft *apple juice*
Apfelsinen *oranges*
Apfelstrudel *apple strudel*
Apfeltasche *apple turnover*
Apfelwein *cider*
Aprikosen *apricots*
Arme Ritter *bread soaked in milk and egg then fried*
Artischocken *artichokes*
Auberginen *eggplants*
Auflauf *sweet or savory gratin dish*
Aufschnitt *cold cuts*
Austern *oysters*

B

Backobst *dried fruit*
Backpflaume *prune*
Baiser *meringue*
Balkansalat *cabbage and pepper salad*
Bananen *bananas*
Bandnudeln *ribbon noodles*
Basilikum *basil*
Bauernauflauf *bacon and potato omelet*
Bauernfrühstück *fried potato, bacon ,and egg*
Bauernomelett *bacon and potato omelet*
Bechamelkartoffeln *potatoes in a creamy sauce*
Beckenoffe *layered meat and potato casserole*
Bedienung *service*
Beilagen *side dishes*
Berliner *jam doughnut*
Bier *beer*
Birnen *pears*
Biskuit *sponge cake*
Bismarckhering *filleted pickled herring*
Blätterteig *puff pastry*
blau *cooked in vinegar; virtually raw (as in steak cooked "bleu")*
Blumenkohl *cauliflower*
blutig *rare (as in steak)*
Blutwurst *black pudding*
Bockwurst *large frankfurter sausage*
Bohnen *beans*
Bouillon *clear soup*
Braten *roast meat*
Brathering *pickled and fried herring, served cold*
Bratkartoffeln *fried potatoes*
Bratwurst *grilled pork sausage*
Brot *bread*
Brötchen *roll*
Brühwurst *large frankfurter*

Brust *breast*
Bückling *smoked red herring*
Buletten *burgers; rissoles*
Bunte Platte *mixed platter*
Burgundersoße *Burgundy wine sauce*
Buttercremetorte *cream cake*
Buttermilch *buttermilk*

C

Champignons *mushrooms*
Cordon bleu *veal cordon bleu*
Currywurst mit Pommes *curried pork sausage with fries*

D

Dampfnudeln *sweet yeast dumpling*
Deutsches Beefsteak *minced meat or patty*
Dicke Bohnen *fava beans*
Dillsoße *dill sauce*
durchgebraten *well-done*
durchwachsen *with fat*
durchwachsener Speck *streaky bacon*

E

Eier *eggs*
Eierauflauf *omelet*
Eierkuchen *pancake*
Eierspeise *scrambled eggs*
eingelegt *pickled*
Eintopf *stew*
Eintopfgericht *stew*
Eis *ice*
Eisbecher *sundae*
Eisbein *knuckle of pork*
Eisschokolade *iced chocolate*
Eissplittertorte *ice chip cake*
Endiviensalat *endive salad*
englisch *rare*
Entenbraten *roast duck*

entgrätet *boned (fish)*
Erbsen *peas*
Erdbeertorte *strawberry cake*
Essig *vinegar*

F

Falscher Hase *meat loaf*
Fasan *pheasant*
Fenchel *fennel*
Fett *fat*
Filet *fillet (steak)*
Fisch *fish*
Fischfrikadellen *fishcakes*
Fischstäbchen *fish fingers*
Flädlesuppe *consommé with pancake strips*
flambiert *flambéed*
Fleischbrühe *bouillon*
Fleischkäse *meat loaf*
Fleischklößchen *meatball(s)*
Fleischpastete *meat vol-au-vent*
Fleischsalat *diced meat salad with mayonnaise*
Fleischwurst *pork sausage*
Fond *meat juices*
Forelle *trout*
Forelle Müllerin (Art) *pan-fried trout with butter and lemon*
Frikadelle *rissole*
Frikassee *fricassee*
frittiert *(deep-) fried*
Froschschenkel *frog's legs*
Fruchtsaft *fruit juice*
Frühlingsrolle *spring roll*

G

Gans *goose*
Gänseleberpastete *goose-liver pâté*
garniert *garnished*
Gebäck *pastries, cakes*
gebacken *baked*

gebraten *roast*
gedünstet *steamed*
Geflügel *poultry*
Geflügelleberragout *chicken liver ragoût*
gefüllt *stuffed*
gefüllte Kalbsbrust *stuffed breast of veal*
gekocht *boiled*
Gelee *jelly*
gemischter Salat *mixed salad*
Gemüse *vegetable(s)*
Gemüseplatte *assorted vegetables*
gepökelt *salted, pickled*
geräuchert *smoked*
Gericht *dish*
geschmort *braised, stewed*
Geschnetzeltes *strips of fried meat in cream sauce*
gespickt *larded*
Getränke *beverages*
Gewürze *spices*
Gewürzgurken *gherkins*
Goldbarsch *type of perch*
Götterspeise *jelly*
gratiniert *au gratin*
Grieß *semolina*
Grießklößchen *semolina dumplings*
grüne Bohnen *green beans*
grüne Nudeln *green pasta*
grüner Aal *fresh eel*
Grünkohl *(curly) kale*
Gulasch *goulash*
Gulaschsuppe *goulash soup*
Gurkensalat *cucumber salad*

H, I

Hackfleisch *mince*
Hähnchen *chicken*
Hähnchenkeule *chicken leg*
Haifischflossensuppe *shark-fin soup*

Hammelbraten *roast mutton*
Hammelfleisch *mutton*
Hammelkeule *leg of mutton*
Hammelrücken *saddle of mutton*
Handkäs mit Musik *strong cheese in a salad dressing*
Hartkäse *hard cheese*
Haschee *hash*
Hasenkeule *haunch of hare*
Hasenpfeffer *hare casserole*
Hauptspeisen *main courses*
Hecht *pike*
Heidelbeeren *bilberries, blueberries*
Heilbutt *halibut*
Heringsstipp *herring salad*
Heringstopf *pickled herrings in sauce*
Herz *heart*
Herzragout *heart ragoût*
Himbeeren *raspberries*
Himmel und Erde *potato and apple purée with black pudding or liver sausage*
Hirn *brains*
Hirschbraten *roast venison*
Honig *honey*
Honigmelone *honeydew melon*
Hoppelpoppel *bacon and potato omelet*
Hüfte *haunch*
Huhn *chicken*
Hühnerbrühe *chicken broth*
Hühnerfrikassee *chicken fricassee*
Hülsenfrüchte *peas and beans, legumes*
Hummer *lobster*
Ingwer *ginger*

J, K

Jägerschnitzel *cutlet with mushrooms*
Kabeljau *cod*
Kaffee *coffee*

Kaiserschmarrn *scrambled crepe with raisins*
Kakao *cocoa*
Kalbfleisch *veal*
Kalbsbries *sweetbread*
Kalbsfrikassee *veal fricassee*
Kalbshaxe *leg of veal*
Kalbsnierenbraten *roast veal with kidney*
Kalbsschnitzel *veal cutlet*
kalte Platte *cold platter*
kaltes Büfett *cold buffet*
Kaltschale *cold, sweet fruit soup*
Kaninchen *rabbit*
Kapern *capers*
Karamellpudding *caramel blancmange*
Karotten *carrots*
Karpfen *carp*
Kartoffelbrei *mashed potato*
Kartoffeln *potatoes*
Kartoffelpuffer *potato fritters*
Kartoffelpüree *mashed potato*
Kartoffelsalat *potato salad*
Käse *cheese*
Käsegebäck *cheese savouries*
Käsekuchen *cheesecake*
Käseplatte *selection of cheeses*
Käse-Sahne-Torte *cream cheesecake*
Käsespätzle *home-made noodles with cheese*
Kasseler Rippenspeer *smoked pork loin*
Kasserolle *casserole*
Kassler *smoked pork loin*
Kastanien *chestnuts*
Katenrauchwurst *smoked sausage*
Keule *leg, haunch*
Kieler Sprotten *smoked sprats*
Kirschen *cherries*

klare Brühe *consommé*
Klöße *dumplings*
Knäckebrot *crispbread*
Knacker *pork sausage for boiling or frying*
Knackwurst *pork sausage for boiling or frying*
Knoblauch *garlic*
Knochen *bone*
Knochenschinken *ham on the bone*
Knödel *dumplings*
Kognak *brandy*
Kohl *cabbage*
Kohlrouladen *stuffed cabbage leaves*
Kohl und Pinkel *cabbage, potatoes, sausage, and smoked meat*
Kompott *stewed fruit*
Konfitüre *jam*
Königinpastete *chicken vol-au-vent*
Königsberger Klopse *meatballs in caper sauce*
Königskuchen *type of fruit cake*
Kopfsalat *lettuce*
Kotelett *chop*
Krabben *shrimps; prawns*
Krabbencocktail *shrimp cocktail*
Kraftbrühe *beef consommé*
Kräuter *herbs*
Krautsalat *coleslaw*
Krautwickel *stuffed cabbage leaves*
Krebs *crayfish*
Kresse *cress*
Kroketten *croquettes*
Kruste *crust*

Kuchen *cake*
Kümmel *caraway seeds*
Kürbis *pumpkin*

L

Labskaus *meat, fish, and potato stew*
Lachs *salmon*
Lachsersatz *cold smoked pollack (fish) dyed to look like salmon*
Lachsforelle *sea trout*
Lachsschinken *smoked rolled fillet of ham*
Lamm *lamb*
Lammrücken *saddle of lamb*
Langusten *spiny lobsters*
Lauch *leek*
Leber *liver*
Leberkäse *baked pork and beef loaf*
Leberpastete *liver pâté*
Leberwurst *liver pâté*
Lebkuchen *gingerbread*
Leinsamenbrot *linseed bread*
Leipziger Allerlei *mixed vegetables*
Linsen *lentils*

M

mager *lean*
Mehrkornbrot *multigrain bread*
Majoran *marjoram*
Makrele *mackerel*
Makronen *macaroons*
Mandeln *almonds*
mariniert *marinaded, pickled*
Markklößchen *marrow dumplings*
Marmelade *jam*
Maronen *sweet chestnuts*
Matjes(hering) *young herring*
Medaillons *small fillets*
Meeresfische *seafish*
Meeresfrüchte *seafood*

Meerrettich *horseradish*
Miesmuscheln *mussels*
Milch *milk*
Milchmixgetränk *milk shake*
Milchreis *rice pudding*
Mineralwasser *mineral water*
Mohnkuchen *poppyseed cake*
Möhren *carrots*
Mohrrüben *carrots*
Most *fruit wine*
Mus *purée*
Muscheln *mussels*
Muskat(nuss) *nutmeg*
MWSt (Mehrwertsteuer) *VAT*

N

nach Art des Hauses *house special*
nach Hausfrauenart *home-made*
Nachspeisen *desserts*
Nachtisch *dessert*
Napfkuchen *ring-shaped poundcake*
natürlich *natural*
Nieren *kidneys*
Nudeln *pasta, noodles*
Nüsse *nuts*

O

Obstsalat *fruit salad*
Ochsenschwanzsuppe *oxtail soup*
Öl *oil*
Oliven *olives*
Orangen *oranges*
Orangensaft *orange juice*

P

Palatschinken *filled pancakes*
paniert *breaded*
Paprika *peppers, paprika*
Paprikaschoten *peppers*

Paradiesäpfel *tomatoes*
Pastete *vol-au-vent*
Pellkartoffeln *potatoes boiled in their jackets*
Petersilie *parsley*
Pfannkuchen *crepe(s)*
Pfeffer *pepper*
Pfifferlinge *chanterelles*
Pfirsiche *peaches*
Pflaumen *plums*
Pflaumenkuchen *plum tart*
Pflaumenmus *plum jam*
Pichelsteiner Topf *vegetable stew with beef*
pikant *spicy*
Pilze *mushrooms*
Platte *selection*
pochiert *poached*
Pökelfleisch *salt meat*
Pommes frites *French fried potatoes*
Porree *leek*
Potthast *braised beef with sauce*
Poularde *large chicken*
Preiselbeeren *cranberries*
Presskopf *brawn*
Pumpernickel *black rye bread*
Püree *purée, e.g. mashed potato*
püriert *puréed*
Putenschenkel *turkey leg*
Puter *turkey*

Q, R

Quark *curd cheese*
Radieschen *radishes*
Rahm *(sour) cream*
Räucheraal *smoked eel*
Räucherhering *kipper, smoked herring*
Räucherlachs *smoked salmon*
Räucherspeck *smoked bacon*
Rauchfleisch *smoked meat*

Rehbraten *roast venison*
Rehgulasch *venison goulash*
Rehkeule *haunch of venison*
Rehrücken *saddle of venison*
Reibekuchen *potato pancake*
Reis *rice*
Reisbrei *creamed rice*
Reisrand *with rice*
Remoulade *mayonnaise flavoured with herbs, mustard, and capers*
Renke *whitefish*
Rettich *radish*
Rhabarber *rhubarb*
Rheinischer Sauerbraten *roast pickled beef*
Rinderbraten *pot roast*
Rinderfilet *fillet steak*
Rinderrouladen *beef olives*
Rinderzunge *ox tongue*
Rindfleisch *beef*
Rippchen *spareribs*
Risi-Pisi *rice and peas*
Roggenbrot *rye bread*
roh *raw*
Rohkostplatte *selection of salads*
Rollmops *rolled-up pickled herring, rollmops*
rosa *rare to medium*
Rosenkohl *Brussels sprouts*
Rosinen *raisins*
Rostbraten *roast*
Rostbratwurst *barbecued sausage*
Rösti *fried potatoes and onions*
Röstkartoffeln *fried potatoes*
Rotbarsch *type of perch*
Rote Bete *beetroot*
rote Grütze *red berry compôte*
Rotkohl *red cabbage*
Rotkraut *red cabbage*
Rotwein *red wine*
Rühreier *scrambled eggs*
Russische Eier *egg mayonnaise*

S

Sahne *cream*
Salate *salads*
Salatplatte *selection of salads*
Salatsoße *salad dressing*
Salz *salt*
Salzburger Nockerl(n)
  sweet soufflé
Salzheringe *salted herrings*
Salzkartoffeln *boiled potatoes*
Salzkruste *salt crust*
Sandkuchen *type of Madeira cake*
sauer *sour*
Sauerbraten *roast pickled beef*
Sauerkraut *pickled white cabbage*
Sauerrahm *sour cream*
Schaschlik *(shish-) kebab*
Schattenmorellen *morello cherries*
Schellfisch *haddock*
Schildkrötensuppe *real turtle soup*
Schillerlocken *hot smoked dogfish*
Schinken *ham*
Schinkenröllchen *rolled ham*
Schlachtplatte *boiled pork and*
  sausages with pickled cabbage
  and boiled potatoes
Schlagsahne *whipped cream*
Schlei *tench*
Schmorbraten *pot roast*
Schnecken *snails*
Schnittlauch *chives*
Schnitzel *breaded escalope*
Schokolade *chocolate*
Scholle *plaice*
Schulterstück *shoulder piece*
Schupfnudeln *pasta made*
  from potatoes and flour
Schwarzbrot *dark rye bread*
Schwarzwälder Kirschtorte
  Black Forest gâteau
Schwarzwurzeln *salsify*
Schwein *pig*
Schweinebauch *belly of pork*

Schweinefleisch *pork*
Schweinerippe *cured pork chop*
Schweinerollbraten *rolled*
  roast of pork
Schweineschmorbraten
  pot roast pork
Schweineschnitzel
  breaded pork cutlet
Schweinshaxe *knuckle of pork*
Seelachs *pollack (fish)*
Seezunge *sole*
Sekt *sparkling wine*
Sellerie *celeriac, celery*
Semmel *bread roll*
Senf *mustard*
Senfsahnesoße *creamy*
  mustard sauce
Senfsoße *mustard sauce*
Serbisches Reisfleisch *paprika*
  rice with cubed pork, peppers,
  and onions
Soleier *pickled eggs*
Soße *sauce, gravy*
Soufflé *soufflé*
Spanferkel *suckling pig*
Spargel *asparagus*
Spätzle *home-made pasta noodles*
Speck *fatty bacon*
Speisekarte *menu*
Spezialität des Hauses
  house specialty
Spiegeleier *fried eggs*
Spießbraten *joint roasted on a spit*
Spinat *spinach*
Spitzkohl *white cabbage*
Springerle *cookies*
Sprotten *sprats*
Sprudel(wasser) *mineral water*
Stachelbeeren *gooseberries*
Stangen(weiß)brot *French bread*
Steinbutt *turbot*
Steinpilze *cep mushrooms*
Stollen *Christmas fruit loaf*

Strammer Max *ham and fried egg on bread*
Streuselkuchen *cake with crumble topping*
Sülze *brawn*
Suppen *soups*
Suppengrün *mixed herbs and vegetables (used in soup)*
süß *sweet*
süß-sauer *sweet-and-sour*
Süßspeisen *sweet dishes*
Süßwasserfische *freshwater fish*
Szegediner Gulasch *goulash with pickled cabbage*

T

Tafelwasser *(still) mineral water*
Tafelwein *table wine*
Tagesgericht *dish of the day*
Tageskarte *menu of the day*
Tagessuppe *soup of the day*
Tatar *steak tartare*
Taube *pigeon*
Tee *tea*
Teigmantel *pastry case*
Thunfisch *tuna*
Tintenfisch *squid*
Tomaten *tomatoes*
Törtchen *tart(s)*
Torte *torte*
Truthahn *turkey*

U, V

überbacken *au gratin*
Ungarisches Gulasch *Hungarian goulash*
ungebraten *not fried*
Vanille *vanilla*
Vanillesoße *vanilla sauce*
verlorene Eier *poached eggs*
Vollkornbrot *dark whole-grain bread*

vom Grill *grilled*
vom Kalb *veal*
vom Rind *beef*
vom Rost *broiled*
vom Schwein *pork*
Vorspeisen *hors d'oeuvres, starters*

W

Waffeln *waffles*
Waldorfsalat *salad with celery, apples, and walnuts*
Wasser *water*
Wassermelone *watermelon*
Weichkäse *soft cheese*
Weinbergschnecken *snails*
Weinbrand *brandy*
Weincreme *pudding with wine*
Weinschaumcreme *creamed pudding with wine*
Weinsoße *wine sauce*
Weintrauben *grapes*
Weißbier *wheat beer*
Weißbrot *white bread*
Weißkohl *white cabbage*
Weißkraut *white cabbage*
Weißwein *white wine*
Weißwurst *veal sausage*
Weizenbier *fizzy, light-colored beer made with wheat*
Wiener Schnitzel *veal in breadcrumbs*
Wild *game*
Wildschweinkeule *haunch of wild boar*
Wildschweinsteak *wild boar steak*
Windbeutel *cream puff*
Wirsing *savoy cabbage*
Wurst *sausage*
Würstchen *frankfurter(s)*
Wurstplatte *selection of sausages*
Wurstsalat *sausage salad*
Wurstsülze *sausage brawn*
würzig *spicy*

Z

Zander *pike-perch, zander*
Zigeunerschnitzel *veal escalope
    with peppers, mushrooms,
    and onions in tomato sauce*
Zimt *cinnamon*
Zitrone *lemon*
Zitronencreme *lemon cream*
Zucchini *zucchini*
Zucker *sugar*
Zuckererbsen *snow pea*

Zunge *tongue*
Zungenragout *tongue ragoût*
Zutaten *ingredients*
Zwetche/Zwetschge
    type of plum
Zwiebelbrot *onion bread*
Zwiebeln *onions*
Zwiebelringe *onion rings*
Zwiebelsuppe *onion soup*
Zwiebeltorte *onion tart*
Zwischengerichte *entrées*

The gender of German nouns is shown by the word for "the": **der** (masculine), **die** (feminine), and **das** (neuter). **Die** is also used with plural nouns: **(m pl)**, **(f pl)** and **(n pl)** are used to show their gender. Some nouns change endings; here the masculine form is shown, with the feminine ending in parentheses.

A

à la carte *à la carte*
a little *ein wenig*
a lot *viel*
about *etwa*
above *über*
accident *der Unfall*
accommodation *Unterkunft*
account number
  die Kontonummer
across *über*
activities *die Aktivitäten (f pl)*
actor *der Schauspieler*
actress *die Schauspielerin*
adapter *der Adapter*
add (verb) *addieren*
address *die Adresse*
adhesive bandage *das Pflaster*
adhesive tape *der Klebestreifen*
adult *der Erwachsene*
aerobics *das Aerobic*
airplane *das Flugzeug*
after *nach*
afternoon *der Nachmittag*
aftersun lotion *die After-Sun-Lotion*
again *wieder*
airbag *der Airbag*
air-conditioning *die Klimaanlage*
aircraft *das Flugzeug*
airmail *die Luftpost*
airport *der Flughafen*

aisle *der Gang*
aisle seat *der Gangplatz*
alarm clock *der Wecker*
alcoholic drinks *die alkoholischen Getränke (n pl)*
all *alle(s)*
allergic *allergisch*
allergy *die Allergie*
almost *fast*
alone *allein*
along *entlang*
already *bereits*
alright *in Ordnung*
altitude *die Höhe*
always *immer*
ambulance *der Krankenwagen*
amount *der Betrag*
amusement park *der Erlebnispark*
and *und*
angry *verärgert*
animals *die Tiere (n pl)*
ankle *der Knöchel*
another (different) *andere*
another (one more) *noch ein(e) (n)*
answer (verb) *antworten*
answering machine *der Anrufbeantworter*
antibiotics *die Antibiotika (n pl)*
antiseptic *das Antiseptikum*
anything *irgendetwas*

apartment *die Wohnung*
apartment block *der Wohnblock*
appearance *die äußere Erscheinung*
appetizer *die Vorspeise*
applaud (verb) *applaudieren*
apple *der Apfel*
apple juice *der Apfelsaft*
application *die Anwendung*
appointment *der Termin*
apricot *die Aprikose*
April *der April*
apron *die Schürze*
arc *der Bogen*
arch *das Gewölbe*
architect *Architekt(in) (m/f)*
architecture *die Architektur*
area *die Fläche*
arm *der Arm*
armband; bracelet *das Armband*
arm rest *die Armlehne*
around *um*
arrivals *die Ankunft*
arrivals hall *die Ankunftshalle*
arrive (verb) *ankommen*
art *die Kunst*
art gallery *das Kunstmuseum*
arthritis *die Arthrose*
artificial sweetener *der Süßstoff*
artist *Künstler(in) (m/f)*
as (like) *wie*
ashtray *der Aschenbecher*
assistant *die Assistentin*
asthma *das Asthma*
at *auf; an; in*
athlete *Leichtathlet(in) (m/f)*
ATM *der Geldautomat*
attachment *der Anhang*
attack *der Angriff*
attend (verb) *teilnehmen*
attractions *die Sehenswürdigkeiten (f pl)*
audience *das Publikum*

audio guide *der Audioführer*
August *der August*
aunt *die Tante*
Australia *Australien*
automatic *mit Automatik*
automatic payment *der Einzugsauftrag*
automatic ticket machine *der Fahrscheinautomat*
avenue *die Allee*
avocado *die Avocado*
awful *furchtbar*

B

baby *das Baby*
baby changing room *der Wickelraum*
babysitting *das Babysitten*
back *die Lehne*
back (body) *der Rücken*
back (not front of) *die Rückseite*
backpack *der Rucksack*
bacon *der Frühstücksspeck*
bad *schlecht*
badminton *das Badminton*
bag *die Tasche*
bagel *der Bagel*
baggage *das Gepäck*
baggage allowance *das Freigepäck*
baggage claim *die Gepäckausgabe*
baguette *das Baguette*
bake (verb) *backen*
baker *Bäcker(in) (m/f)*
bakery *die Bäckerei*
balcony; gallery *der Balkon*
ball *der Ball*
ballet *das Ballett*
banana *die Banane*
bandage *der Verband*
bank *die Bank*

bank account *das Bankkonto*
bank charge *die Bankgebühr*
bank manager
der Bankdirektor
bank transfer
die Überweisung
bar *die Bar*
bar snacks *die Knabbereien*
barbecue *der Grill*
barbecue *der Grill*
barber *der Herrenfriseur*
bartender *der Barkeeper*
baseball *das Baseball*
baseball mitt *der*
Baseballhandschuh
basement *das Kellergeschoss*
basil *das Basilikum*
basket *der Korb*
basketball *das Basketball*
bathing cap *die Badekappe*
bath robe *der Bademantel*
bathroom *das Badezimmer*
bath towel *das Badetuch*
bathtub *die Badewanne*
battery *die Batterie*
be (verb) *sein*
be lost (verb) *sich verirren*
beach *der Strand*
beach ball *der Strandball*
beach umbrella
der Sonnenschirm
beans *die Bohnen (f pl)*
bear *der Bär*
beautiful *schön*
bed *das Bett*
bed and breakfast *die*
Übernachtung mit Frühstück
bed linen *die Bettwäsche*
bedroom *das Schlafzimmer*
bee *die Biene*
beef *das Rindfleisch*
beer *das Bier*
beet *die Rote Bete*

beetle *der Käfer*
before *vor*
begin (verb) *beginnen*
beginner *Anfänger(in) (m/f)*
beginning *der Anfang*
behind *hinter*
bell *die Klingel*
below *unter*
belt *der Gürtel*
bench *die Bank*
beneath *unterhalb*
berry *die Beere*
beside *neben*
better *besser*
between *zwischen*
beyond *jenseits*
bicycle *das Fahrrad*
bidet *das Bidet*
big *groß*
bike rack *der Fahrradständer*
bikini *der Bikini*
bill (note) *die Note*
birds *die Vögel (m pl)*
birth *die Geburt*
birth certificate *die*
Geburtsurkunde
birthday *der Geburtstag*
bit *das Gebiss*
bite *der Biss*
bitter *bitter*
black *schwarz*
black coffee
der schwarze Kaffee
black tea *Schwarztee*
blackberry *die Brombeere*
blackcurrant *die schwarze*
Johannisbeere
blanket *die Decke*
bleeding *die Blutung*
blender *der Mixer*
blister *die Blase*
block *der Block*
blonde *blond*

blood pressure *der Blutdruck*
blood test *die Blutprobe*
blouse *die Bluse*
blow dry (verb) *föhnen*
blow-dryer *der Föhn*
blue *blau*
blueberry *die Heidelbeere*
blush *das Puderrouge*
board (verb) *an Bord gehen*
boarding gate *der Flugsteig*
boarding pass *die Bordkarte*
boat *das Schiff*
boat trip *die Schifffahrt*
body *der Körper*
body lotion *die Körperlotion*
boil (verb) *kochen*
book *das Buch*
book (verb) *buchen*
book a flight (verb) *einen Flug buchen*
bookstore *der Buchladen*
boot (footwear) *der Stiefel*
bored *gelangweilt*
borrow (verb) *ausleihen*
bottle *die Flasche*
bottle opener *der Flaschenöffner*
bottled water *das Flaschenwasser*
boutique *die Boutique*
bowl *die Schüssel*
bowling *das Bowling*
box *die Schachtel*
box office *die Kasse*
boy *der Junge*
boyfriend *der Freund*
brain *das Gehirn*
brake *die Bremse*
branch *der Ast*
bread *das Brot*
breakdown *die Panne*
breakfast *das Frühstück*
breakfast buffet *das Frühstücksbuffet*

breakfast cereals *die Getreideflocken (f pl)*
brick *der Ziegelstein*
bridge *die Brücke*
briefcase *die Aktentasche*
briefs *der Slip*
brioche *die Brioche*
British *britisch*
broccoli *der Brokkoli*
broil *grillen*
broken *gebrochen*
brooch *die Brosche*
broom *der Besen*
brother *der Bruder*
brown *braun*
brown rice *der Naturreis*
browse (verb) *browsen*
bruise *die Prellung*
brunette *brünett*
bubblebath *das Schaumbad*
bucket *der Eimer*
buckle *die Gürtelschnalle*
buffet *das Buffet*
build (verb) *bauen*
bulb *die Zwiebel*
bulletin board *die Pinnwand*
bumper *die Stoßstange*
bun *das Teilchen*
bunch *der Strauß*
buoy *die Boje*
burger *der Hamburger*
burgle (verb) *einbrechen*
burn (med.) *die Verbrennung*
bus *der Bus*
bus driver *Busfahrer(in) (m/f)*
bus station *der Busbahnhof*
bus stop *die Bushaltestelle*
bus ticket *der Fahrschein*
business *das Geschäft*
bust *die Büste*
but *aber*
butcher *Metzger(in) (m/f)*

butter *die Butter*
butternut squash
  der Butternusskürbis
button *der Knopf*
buy (verb) *kaufen*
by *bis*

C

cab *die Fahrerkabine*
cable *das Kabel*
cable car *die Seilbahn*
cable television
  das Kabelfernsehen
café *das Café*
cakes *das Gebäck*
calculator *der Taschenrechner*
calendar *der Kalender*
call button *der Rufknopf*
calm *ruhig*
camera *die Kamera*
camera bag *die Kameratasche*
camera case *die Kameratasche*
camisole *das Mieder*
camp (verb) *kampieren*
camper van *der Wohnwagen*
camper van site
  der Wohnwagenplatz
camping kettle *der Wasserkocher*
camping stove *der Gaskocher*
campsite *der Campingplatz*
can (noun) *die Dose*
can (verb) *können*
Canada *Kanada*
candy *die Bonbons (n pl)*
canoe *das Kanu*
can opener *der Dosenöffner*
capital *die Hauptstadt*
cappuccino *der Cappuccino*
capsule *die Kapsel*
car *das Auto*
car accident *der*
  Autounfall
car crash *der Verkehrsunfall*

car rental *die*
  Autovermietung
car stereo
  das Autoradio
car wash *die*
  Autowaschanlage
cards *die Karten (f pl)*
cardboard *die Pappe*
cardigan *die Strickjacke*
carnival *der Karneval*
carpet *der Teppich*
carrot *die Karotte*
carry (verb) *tragen*
carry out *zum Mitnehmen*
cart *der Kofferkuli*
carton *die Tüte*
case *das Futteral*
cash *das Bargeld*
cash (verb) *einlösen*
cash machine *der*
  Geldautomat
cash register *die Kasse*
casino *das Kasino*
castle *das Schloss*
casual *leger*
cat *die Katze*
catch (verb) *fangen*
cathedral *der Dom*
cauliflower *der Blumenkohl*
caution *Achtung*
cave *die Höhle*
CD *die CD*
ceiling *die Decke*
celebration *die Feier*
cell phone *das Handy*
center *das Zentrum*
central heating
  die Zentralheizung
cereal *die Getreideflocken (f pl)*
chair *der Stuhl*
chair lift *der Sessellift*
champagne *der Champagner*
change *das Kleingeld*

change (money) *wechseln*
change (verb) *umsteigen*
change purse *der Geldbeutel*
channel *der Kanal*
channel (TV) *der Fernsehkanal*
charge *die Anklage*
charge (verb) *berechnen; verlangen*
cheap *billig*
check *die Rechnung*
check *der Scheck*
checkbook *das Scheckbuch*
check card *die Scheckkarte*
checker *Kassierer(in) (m/f)*
check in (verb) *einchecken*
check-in desk *der Abfertigungsschalter*
checking account *das Girokonto*
checkout (supermarket) *die Kasse*
checkup *der Check-up*
cheek *die Wange*
cheers! *prost!*
cheese *der Käse*
chef *der Küchenchef*
cherry *die Kirsche*
cherry tomato *die Kirschtomate*
chest *die Brust*
chewing gum *der Kaugummi*
chicken *das Hähnchen*
child *das Kind*
child seat *der Kindersitz*
children *die Kinder (n pl)*
chili pepper *die Peperoni (f pl)*
chill *die Verkühlung*
chin *das Kinn*
chocolate *die Praline*
choke (verb) *ersticken*
chop *das Kotelett*
chorizo *die Chorizo*
church *die Kirche*
cigar *die Zigarre*

cigarette *die Zigarette*
cilantro *der Koriander*
cinnamon *der Zimt*
circle *der Kreis*
citrus fruit *die Zitrusfrüchte (f pl)*
city *die (Groß)stadt*
clam *die Venusmuschel*
clean *sauber*
clean (verb) *säubern*
cleaner *die Putzfrau*
cleaning material *das Reinigungsmittel*
client *der Klient*
cliff *die Klippe*
clinic *die Klinik*
clock *die Uhr*
clock radio *der Radiowecker*
close (near) *nah*
close (verb) *schließen*
closed *geschlossen*
closet *der Kleiderschrank*
clothes *die Kleidung*
cloud *die Wolke*
cloudy *bewölkt*
club *das Kreuz*
coach *der Reisebus*
coast *die Küste*
coaster *der Untersetzer*
coast guard *die Küstenwache*
coat *der Mantel*
coat hanger *der Kleiderbügel*
cockroach *die Schabe*
cocktail *der Cocktail*
coconut *die Kokosnuss*
cod *der Kabeljau*
coffee *der Kaffee*
coffee cup *die Kaffeetasse*
coffee machine *die Kaffeemaschine*
coffee table *der Couchtisch*
coin *die Münze*
colander *das Sieb*
cold *die Erkältung*

cold (adj) *kalt*
cold (illness) *der Schnupfen*
collection *die Leerung*
college *die Hochschule*
color *die Farbe*
colored pencil *der Farbstift*
comb *der Kamm*
come (verb) *kommen*
comforter *die Bettdecke*
comic book *der Comic*
company *die Firma*
compartment *das Abteil*
compass *der Kompass*
complain (verb) *sich beschweren*
complaint *die Beschwerde*
computer *der Computer*
concert *das Konzert*
concourse *die Bahnhofshalle*
conditioner *die Pflegespülung*
condom *das Kondom*
confident *selbstsicher*
confused *verwirrt*
constipation *die Verstopfung*
construction site *die Baustelle*
construction worker *der Bauarbeiter*
consul *der Konsul*
consulate *das Konsulat*
consultation *die Konsultation*
contact lenses *die Kontaktlinsen (f pl)*
contact number *die Rufnummer*
container *der Behälter*
contents *der Inhalt*
continent *der Kontinent*
contraception *die Empfängnisverhütung*
cookie *der Keks*
cookie sheet *das Backblech*
cooking *das Kochen*
cooler *die Kühlbox*
copy (verb) *kopieren*
coral reef *das Korallenriff*

core *das Kerngehäuse*
cork *der Korken*
corkscrew *der Korkenzieher*
corn *der Mais*
corner *der Eckball*
correct *richtig*
cotton *die Baumwolle*
cough *der Husten*
cough medicine *das Hustenmedikament*
count (verb) *zählen*
counter *die Spielmarke*
country *das Land*
couple *das Paar*
courier *der Kurier*
course *der Kurs*
courses *die Gänge*
courtyard *der Hof*
cousin *Cousin(e) (m/f)*
cow *die Kuh*
crab *die Krabbe*
cramp *der Krampf*
cream cheese *der Rahmkäse*
crease *die Wurflinie*
credit card *die Kreditkarte*
crêpes *die Pfannkuchen*
crib *das Kinderbett*
crime *das Verbrechen*
croissant *das Croissant*
cross trainer *der Ellipsentrainer*
crushed *zerstoßen*
crust *die Kruste*
cry (verb) *weinen*
crêpes *die Crêpes (f pl)*
cucumber *die Gurke*
cufflinks *die Manschettenknöpfe (m pl)*
cup *die Tasse*
curly *lockig*
currency exchange *die Wechselstube*

curry *das Curry*
curtain *der Vorhang*
cushion *das Sofakissen*
customer *der Kunde*
customs *der Zoll*
cut *der Schnitt*
cutlery *das Besteck*
cutting board *das Hackbrett*
cycle (verb) *Rad fahren*
cycle helmet *der Fahrradhelm*
cycle lane *der Fahrradweg*

D

dairy products *die Milchprodukte (n pl)*
damaged *beschädigt*
dance *die Tanzmusik*
dancing *das Tanzen*
danger *Lebensgefahr*
dark *dunkel*
daughter *die Tochter*
day *der Tag*
day planner *der Terminkalender*
debit card *die EC-Karte*
December *Dezember*
deck chair *der Liegestuhl*
deep *tief*
deep-fried *frittiert*
degrees *die Grade (m pl)*
delayed *verspätet*
delicatessen *der Delikatessenladen*
delicious *köstlich*
delivery *die Entbindung*
dentist *der Zahnarzt*
deodorant *das Deodorant*
department *der Fachbereich*
department store *das Kaufhaus*
departure board *die Abflugtafel*
departure lounge *die Abflughalle*
departures *der Abflug*
departures hall *die Abflughalle*
deposit *die Anzahlung*

desert *die Wüste*
dessert *das Dessert*
destination *das Reiseziel*
detergent *das Waschpulver*
develop (film) *entwickeln*
diabetic *Diabetiker(in) (m/f)*
dial (verb) *wählen*
diaper *die Windel*
diarrhea *der Durchfall*
dictionary *das Wörterbuch*
diesel *der Diesel*
difficult *schwierig*
digital camera *die Digitalkamera*
digital radio *das Digitalradio*
dining car *der Speisewagen*
dining room *das Esszimmer*
dinner *das Abendessen*
directions *Richtungsangaben*
dirty *schmutzig*
disabled parking *der Behindertenparkplatz*
disabled person *die/der Behinderte*
dishes *die Töpferware*
disciplines *die Disziplinen (f pl)*
discuss (verb) *diskutieren*
disembark (verb) *von Bord gehen*
dish *die Schüssel*
dishwasher *die Spülmaschine*
distance *die Entfernung*
district *der Bezirk*
dive (verb) *springen*
divorced *geschieden*
doctor *der Arzt*
doctor's surgery *die Arztpraxis*
dog *der Hund*
doll *die Puppe*
dolphin *der Delfin*

don't *nicht*
door *die Tür*
doorbell *die Türklingel*
dosage *die Dosierung*
double bed *das Doppelbett*
double room *das Doppelzimmer*
down *hinunter*
download (verb) *herunterladen*
drain *der Kanal*
draw (verb) *zeichnen*
drawer *die Schublade*
drawing *die Zeichnung*
dress *das Kleid*
drink (noun) *das Getränk*
drink (verb) *trinken*
drinks *die Getränke (n pl)*
drive (verb) *fahren*
driver *Fahrer(in) (m/f)*
driving license *der Führerschein*
drugstore *die Apotheke*
dry *trocken*
duck *die Ente*
duffel bag *die Reisetasche*
during *während*
dust pan *das Kehrblech*
duty-free store *der Duty Free Shop*
DVD *die DVD*
DVD player *der DVD-Spieler*

E

each *jede(r)(s)*
ear *das Ohr*
early *früh*
earring *der Ohrring*
earthquake *das Erdbeben*
east *der Osten*
easy *leicht*

eat (verb) *essen*
eat-in *hier essen*
eating out *auswärts essen*
egg *das Ei*
eggplant *die Aubergine*
eight *acht*
elbow *der Ellbogen*
electric razor *der Rasierapparat*
electrician *der Elektriker*
electricity *der Strom*
elevator *der Lift*
email *die E-Mail*
email address *die E-Mail-Adresse*
embarrassed *verlegen*
embassy *die Botschaft*
emergency *der Notfall*
emergency exit *der Notausgang*
emergency room *die Notaufnahme*
emergency services *die Notdienste (m pl)*
emigrate (verb) *emigrieren*
empty *leer*
end *das Ende*
engaged/busy *besetzt*
engine *der Motor*
English *Engländer(in) (m/f)*
English (language) *Englisch*
engraving *der Stich*
enjoy (verb) *genießen*
entrance *der Eingang*
entrance ticket *die Eintrittskarte*
envelope *der Briefumschlag*
epileptic *Epileptiker(in) (m/f)*
equipment *die Ausrüstung*
espresso *der Espresso*
euro *der Euro*
evening *der Abend*
evening menu *das Abendmenü*

every *jeder*
exactly *genau*
examination *die Untersuchung*
examine (verb) *untersuchen*
exchange rate
  der Wechselkurs
excited *begeistert*
excursion *der Ausflug*
excuse me *Entschuldigung*
exercise bike *der Heimtrainer*
exhaust (car) *der Auspuff*
exhibition *die Ausstellung*
exit *der Ausgang*
expensive *teuer*
expiration date
  das Verfallsdatum
express service
  der Express-Service
extension cord *das
  Verlängerungskabel*
extra *extra*
eye *das Auge*
eyebrow *die Augenbraue*
eyelash *die Wimper*
eyeliner *der Eyeliner*

F

fabric *der Stoff*
face *das Gesicht*
faint (verb) *in Ohnmacht fallen*
fairground *der Rummelplatz*
fall *der Herbst*
family *die Familie*
family room *das Familienzimmer*
family ticket *die Familienkarte*
fan *der Ventilator*
far *weit*
fare *der Fahrpreis*
farm *der Bauernhof*
farmer *der Landwirt*
fashion *die Mode*
fast *schnell*
fast food *der Schnellimbiss*

fat *das Fett*
father *der Vater*
faucet *der Wasserhahn*
February *Februar*
feel (verb) *fühlen*
female *die Frau*
fence *der Zaun*
ferry *die Fähre*
festivals *die Feste (f pl)*
fever *das Fieber*
field *das Feld*
fill (verb) *füllen*
fillet *das Filet*
find (verb) *finden*
fine (legal) *die Strafe*
finger *der Finger*
finish (verb) *beenden*
fins *die Flossen (f pl)*
fire *der Brand*
fire alarm *der Feueralarm*
fire department *die Feuerwehr*
fire engine *das Feuerwehrauto*
fire escape *die Feuertreppe*
fire extinguisher *der
  Feuerlöscher*
firefighter *der
  Feuerwehrmann*
first *erste*
first aid *die Erste Hilfe*
first-aid box *der
  Erste-Hilfe-Kasten*
fish *die Fische*
fishing *das Angeln*
fishing rod *die Angelrute*
fish seller
  Fischhändler(in) (m/f)
fitness *die Fitness*
fitting room
  die Umkleidekabine
five *fünf*
fix (verb) *befestigen; festlegen*
flag *die Fahne*
flash gun *das Blitzgerät*

flashlight *die Taschenlampe*
flash photography *das Fotografieren mit Blitzlicht*
flat *flach*
flat tire *die Reifenpanne*
flight *der Flug*
flight attendant *Flugbegleiter(in) (m/f)*
flight connection *die Flugverbindung*
flight number *die Flugnummer*
flip-flops *die Flip-Flops (m pl)*
float *das Schwimmkissen*
flood *die Überschwemmung*
floor *der Fußboden*
florist *Florist(in) (m/f)*
flower arrangements *Blumenarrangements (n pl)*
flowers *die Blumen (f pl)*
flu *die Grippe*
fly (verb) *fliegen*
food *das Essen*
foot *der Fuß*
footpath *der Fußweg*
for *für*
foreign currency *die ausländische Währung*
forest *der Wald*
fork *die Gabel*
forget (verb) *vergessen*
form *die Form*
forward *der Mittelstürmer*
fountain *der Springbrunnen*
four *vier*
fracture *der Bruch*
fragile *zerbrechlich*
frame *das Gestänge*
free *frei*
French press *die Cafetière*
fresh *frisch*
Friday *Freitag*
fried *gebraten*

friend *Freund(in) (m/f)*
from *von; aus*
front door *die Haustür*
frost *der Frost*
frozen *tiefgefroren*
fruit *das Obst*
fry (verb) *braten*
frying pan *die Bratpfanne*
fuel gauge *die Benzinuhr*
full *voll*
furniture store *das Möbelgeschäft*
fuse box *der Sicherungskasten*

G

game *das Spiel*
garage *die Werkstatt*
garbage *der Müll*
garbage can *die Mülltonne*
garden *der Garten*
garlic *der Knoblauch*
gas *das Gas*
gasoline *das Benzin*
gas station *die Tankstelle*
gate *das Tor*
gearshift *die Kupplung*
gem stone *der Edelstein*
get (verb) *bekommen*
gift *das Geschenk*
gift store *die Geschenkboutique*
gift-wrap (verb) *als Geschenk verpacken*
gin *der Gin*
ginger *der Ingwer*
giraffe *die Giraffe*
girl *das Mädchen*
girlfriend *die Freundin*
give (verb) *geben*
glass *das Glas*
glasses *die Brille*
gloss *der Glanz*

gloves *die Handschuhe (f pl)*
glue *der Klebstoff*
go (verb) *gehen*
go for a walk (verb) *spazieren gehen*
go out (verb) *ausgehen*
go shopping (verb) *einkaufen gehen*
goggles *die Schutzbrille*
gold *das Gold*
golf *das Golfspiel*
golf ball *der Golfball*
golf club *der Golfclub*
golf course *der Golfplatz*
golf tee *das Golf-Tee*
good *gut*
good afternoon *Guten Tag*
goodbye *Auf Wiedersehen!*
good day *Guten Tag!*
good evening *Guten Abend!*
good morning *Guten Morgen!*
good night *Gute Nacht!*
gram *das Gramm*
grater *die Reibe*
gray *grau*
Great Britain *Großbritannien*
green *grün*
green tea *der Grüntee*
griddle pan *die Grillpfanne*
groceries *die Lebensmittel*
ground *gemahlen*
group *die Gruppe*
guarantee *die Garantie*
guest *der Gast*
guide *der Führer*
guidebook *der Reiseführer*
guided tour *die Besichtigungstour*
gym *das Fitnessstudio*

H

hail *der Hagel*
hair *das Haar*
hair colors *die Haarfarben (f pl)*
hairdresser's *der Frisiersalon*
half *die Hälfte*
hand *die Hand*
handbag *die Handtasche*
handle *der Griff*
hand luggage *das Handgepäck*
happen (verb) *geschehen*
happy *froh*
harbor *der Hafen*
hard *hart*
hardware store *das Haushaltswarengeschäft*
hat *der Hut*
hatchback *das Hecktürmodell*
hate (verb) *hassen*
have (verb) *haben*
hay fever *der Heuschnupfen*
hazard lights *die Warnleuchten (f pl)*
he *er*
head *der Kopf*
headache *die Kopfschmerzen*
headlight *der Scheinwerfer*
headphones *die Kopfhörer*
head rest *die Kopfstütze*
health *die Gesundheit*
health insurance *die Krankenversicherung*
hear (verb) *hören*
heart *das Herz*
heart condition *die Herzkrankheit*
heater *der Heizlüfter*
heating *die Heizung*
heavy *schwer*
heel (foot) *die Ferse*
height *die Höhe*
hello *Hallo!*

help (noun) *Hilfe*
help (verb) *helfen*
her *ihr(e)*
herb *das Kraut*
here *hier*
high blood pressure
  der hohe Blutdruck
high chair *der Kinderstuhl*
high-speed-train *der
  Hochgeschwindigkeitszug*
highway *die Autobahn*
hiking *das Wandern*
hiking boots
  die Wanderschuhe (m pl)
hill *der Hügel*
hip *die Hüfte*
hockey *das Hockey*
hold (verb) *halten*
home *das Heim*
hood *die Kapuze*
hood (car) *die Mütze*
horn (car) *die Hupe*
horse *das Pferd*
horseback riding *das Reiten*
hospital *das
  Krankenhaus*
host *der Gastgeber*
hot *heiß*
hot (spicy) *scharf*
hot chocolate *die heiße
  Schokolade*
hot drinks *die heißen
  Getränke (n pl)*
hotel *das Hotel*
hour *die Stunde*
house *das Haus*
hovercraft *das
  Hovercraft*
how many? *wie viel(e)?*
how? *wie?*
humid *feucht*
hurricane *der Hurrikan*
hurry (verb) *beeilen*

husband *der Ehemann*
hydrant *der Hydrant*
hydrofoil *das Tragflügelboot*

I

I *ich*
ice *das Eis*
ice-skating *das Eislaufen*
icy *eisig*
ID *der Ausweis*
immigration *die
  Einwanderung*
inbox *der
  Posteingang*
inch *der Zoll*
infection *die Infektion*
in-flight meal
  die Flugmahlzeit
in front of *vor*
inhaler *der Inhalator*
injection *die Spritze*
injure (verb) *verletzen*
injury *die Verletzung*
insect repellent *das
  Insektenschutzmittel*
inside *innerhalb*
instructions *die
  Gebrauchsanweisung (f pl)*
insurance *die Versicherung*
insurance company *die
  Versicherungsgesellschaft*
insurance policy *die
  Versicherungspolice*
intensive care unit *die
  Intensivstation*
interesting *interessant*
internet *das Internet*
internet café *das
  Internetcafé*
interpreter
  Dolmetscher(in) (m/f)
into *in*
inventory *das Inventar*

iPod *der iPod*
iron *das Bügeleisen*
ironing board *das Bügelbrett*
island *die Insel*
it *er; sie; es*
Italian *Italiener(in) (m/f)*
Italy *Italien*

J

jacket *die Jacke*
jam *die Konfitüre*
January *Januar*
jar *das Glas*
jaw *der Kiefer*
jazz club *der Jazzclub*
jeans *die Jeans (f pl)*
jellyfish *die Qualle*
jet skiing *das Jetskifahren*
jeweler *Juwelier(in) (m/f)*
jewelry *der Schmuck*
jogging *das Jogging*
juice *der Saft*
July *Juli*
June *Juni*

K

kayak *das Kajak*
keep (verb) *behalten*
ketchup *der Ketchup*
kettle *der Wasserkessel*
key *der Schlüssel*
keyboard *die Tastatur*
kidney *die Niere*
kilo *das Kilo*
kilogram *das Kilogramm*
kilometer *der Kilometer*
kitchen *die Küche*
kitchen shelves *das Küchenregal*
knee *das Knie*
knife *das Messer*

knock down *niederschlagen*
know (facts) *wissen*
know (people) *kennen*

L

lake *der See*
lamb *das Lamm*
laptop *der Laptop*
last *letzte*
last week *letzte Woche*
late *spät*
laugh (verb) *lachen*
laundromat *der Waschsalon*
lawyer *Rechtsanwalt(in) (m/f)*
leak *das Leck*
learn (verb) *lernen*
leave (verb) *verlassen*
left *links*
left (direction) *links*
left luggage *die Gepäcksaufbewahrung*
leg *das Bein*
leisure *die Freizeit*
lemon *die Zitrone*
lemon grass *das Zitronengras*
lemonade *die Limonade*
length *die Länge*
lens *die Linse*
letter carrier *der Briefträger*
lettuce *der Salat*
library *die Bibliothek*
lid *der Deckel*
life jacket *die Schwimmweste*
lifeguard *der Rettungsschwimmer*
life ring *der Rettungsring*
lift pass *der Liftpass*
light (adj) *hell*
light (noun) *das Licht*
light (verb) *beleuchten*
light bulb *die Glühbirne*
lighter *das Feuerzeug*

lighthouse *der Leuchtturm*
lights switch *der Lichtschalter*
lime *die Linde*
liquid cleanser *der Flüssigreiniger*
list *die Liste*
listen (verb) *zuhören*
liter *der Liter*
little *klein*
living room *das Wohnzimmer*
load (verb) *füllen*
loan *die Ausleihe*
local *lokal; örtlich*
lock *das Schloss*
lockers *die Schließfächer (f pl)*
log on (verb) *einloggen*
log out (verb) *ausloggen*
long *lang*
look (verb) *schauen*
lose (verb) *verlieren*
lost property *das Fundamt*
love (sport) *null*
love (verb) *lieben*
low *niedrig*
luggage *das Gepäck*
luggage rack *die Gepäckablage*
lunch *das Mittagessen*
lunch menu *das Mittagsmenü*

M

magazine *die Zeitschrift*
mail *die Post*
mailbox *der Briefkasten*
main course *das Hauptgericht*
make (verb) *machen*
makeup *das Make-up*
male *der Mann*
mallet *der Holzhammer*
man *der Mann*
manager *der Chef*
mango *die Mango*
manicure *die Maniküre*
manual *das Handbuch*

manuscript *das Manuskript*
March *März*
marina *der Jachthafen*
market *der Markt*
marmalade *die Orangenmarmelade*
married *verheiratet*
mascara *die Wimperntusche*
massage *die Massage*
match (light) *das Streichholz*
match (sport) *das Match; das Spiel*
matte *matt*
mattress *die Matratze*
May *Mai*
maybe *vielleicht*
mayonnaise *die Majonäse*
meal *die Mahlzeit*
measure *das Maß*
meat *das Fleisch*
meatballs *die Fleischklöße (m pl)*
mechanic *Mechaniker(in) (m/f)*
medicine *die Medizin*
medium *mittelgroß*
memory card *die Memory Card*
memory stick *der Memory Stick*
message *die Nachricht*
metal *das Metall*
meter *der Meter*
microwave *die Mikrowelle*
middle *die Mitte*
midnight *die Mitternacht*
migraine *die Migräne*
mile *die Meile*
milk *die Milch*
mineral water *das Mineralwasser*
mini bar *die Minibar*
mint *die Minze*
minute *die Minute*
mirror *der Spiegel*
mistake *der Fehler*
misty *nebelig*

mixed *gemischt*
mole *das Muttermal*
Monday *der Montag*
money *das Geld*
monkey *der Affe*
month *der Monat*
monument *das Denkmal*
mop *der Mopp*
more *mehr*
morning *der Morgen*
mosquito *die Stechmücke*
mosquito net *das Moskitonetz*
mother *die Mutter*
motorcycle *das Motorrad*
mountain *der Berg*
mountain bike *das Mountainbike*
mouse *die Maus*
mouse (computer) *die Maus*
mouth *der Mund*
mouthwash *das Mundwasser*
move *der Zug*
movie *der Film*
movie theater *das Kino*
mozzarella *der Mozzarella*
much *viel*
muffin *der Muffin*
mug *der Becher*
muscles *die Muskeln (m pl)*
museum *das Museum*
mushroom *der Pilz*
music *die Musik*
musician *Musiker(in) (m/f)*
must (verb) *müssen*
mustard *der Senf*
my *mein(e)*

N

nail *der Nagel*
nail clippers *die Nagelzange*
nail scissors *die Nagelschere*
name *der Name*
napkin *die Serviette*
narrow *schmal*

national park *der Nationalpark*
natural *das Auflösungszeichen*
nausea *die Übelkeit*
navigate (verb) *navigieren*
near *nah*
neck *der Nacken*
necklace *die Halskette*
need (verb) *brauchen*
nervous *nervös*
net *das Netz*
network *das Netzwerk*
never *nie*
new *neu*
news *die Nachrichten (f pl)*
newspaper *die Zeitung*
next *nächste*
next to *neben (da)*
next week *nächste Woche*
nice *hübsch; angenehm*
night *die Nacht*
nightclub *der Nachtclub*
nine *neun*
no *nein*
no entry *Keine Zufahrt!*
noisy *laut*
noon *der Mittag*
normal *normal*
north *der Norden*
nose *die Nase*
nosebleed *das Nasenbluten*
not *nicht*
notebook *das Notizbuch*
nothing *nichts*
November *der November*
now *jetzt*
number *die Zahl*
number plate *das Nummernschild*
nurse *die Krankenschwester/ der Krankenpfleger*
nuts *die Nüsse (f pl)*

oar *das Ruder*
oats *der Hafer*
occupations *die Berufe (f pl)*
occupied *besetzt*
ocean *der Ozean*
October *Oktober*
octopus *der Krake*
of *von*
off *aus*
office *das Büro*
often *oft*
oil *das Öl*
ointment *die Salbe*
OK *Okay*
old *alt*
olive oil *das Olivenöl*
olives *die Oliven (f pl)*
omelet *das Omelett*
on *auf*
on board *an Bord*
one *eins*
one-way ticket *die Einzelfahrt*
onion *die Zwiebel*
online *Online*
only *nur*
onto *auf*
open *offen*
open (verb) *öffnen*
opening hours *die Öffnungszeiten (f pl)*
opera *die Oper*
opera house *das Opernhaus*
operation *die Operation*
opposite *gegenüber*
or *oder*
orange (color) *orange*
orange juice *der Orangensaft*
order *die Bestellung*
order (verb) *bestellen*
our *unser*
out *aus*
out *ausscheiden*

outside *außerhalb*
oven *der Backofen*
over *über*
overdraft *die Kontoüberziehung*
overhead bin *das Gepäckfach*
owe (verb) *schulden*

P

pack of cards *das Kartenspiel*
pads *die Schutzpolster (n pl)*
pail *der Eimer*
pain *der Schmerz*
painkiller *das Schmerzmittel*
painting *das Gemälde*
pair *das Paar*
pajamas *der Schlafanzug*
pan *die Waagschale*
pan fried *kurzgebraten*
pants *die Hose*
panty hose *die Strumpfhose*
paper *das Papier*
papers (identity) *die Papiere (n pl)*
parcel *das Paket*
parents *die Eltern*
park *der Park*
parka *der Anorak*
parking lot *der Parkplatz*
parking meter *die Parkuhr*
parmesan *der Parmesan*
parsley *die Petersilie*
partner *Partner(in) (m/f)*
pass *der Pass*
pass (verb) *überholen*
passenger *Passagier(in) (m/f)*
passport *der Pass*
passport control *die Passkontrolle*
pasta *die Nudeln*
pastry *das Gebäck*
path *der Weg*
patient *Patient(in) (m/f)*
patient chart *die Patientenkurve*
pause *die Pause*

pay (verb) *zahlen*
pay in (verb) *einzahlen*
payment *die Zahlung*
payphone *der Münzfernsprecher*
peanut *die Erdnuss*
peanut butter *die Erdnussbutter*
pear *die Birne*
pedestrian crossing *der Fußgängerübergang*
pedicure *die Pediküre*
peel (verb) *schälen*
peeler *der Schäler*
pen *der Füller*
pencil *der Bleistift*
people *die Menschen (m pl)*
pepper *der Pfeffer*
perfume *das Parfum*
perhaps *vielleicht*
personal CD player *der CD-Spieler*
pet *das Haustier*
pharmacist *Apotheker(in) (m/f)*
pharmacy *die Apotheke*
phone *das Telefon*
phone card *die Telefonkarte*
photo album *das Fotoalbum*
photo frame *der Fotorahmen*
photograph *das Foto*
photography *die Fotografie*
pianist *Pianist(in) (m/f)*
picnic *das Picknick*
picnic basket *das Picknickkorb*
pie *die Pastete*
piece *das Stück*
pilates *das Pilates*
pill *die Pille; die Tablette*
pillow *das Kopfkissen*
pilot *Pilot(in) (m/f)*
PIN *die Geheimzahl*
pink *rosa*
pint *das Pint*
pitch *die Spielbahn*

pitch a tent (verb) *ein Zelt aufschlagen*
pitcher *der Krug*
pizza *die Pizza*
plane *der Hobel*
planet *der Planet*
plant labels *Pflanzenschildchen (n pl)*
plants *die Pflanzen (f pl)*
plate *der Teller*
platform *der Bahnsteig*
play *das Theaterstück*
play (games) *spielen*
playground *der Spielplatz*
please *bitte*
plug *der Stecker*
plum *die Pflaume*
plumber *Klempner(in) (m/f)*
pocket *die Tasche*
point *der Punkt*
police *die Polizei*
police car *das Polizeiauto*
police officer *Polizist(in) (m/f)*
police station *die Polizeiwache*
pork *das Schweinefleisch*
porridge *der Haferbrei*
porter *der Gepäckträger*
portion *die Portion*
possible *möglich*
post office *das Postamt*
postage *die Portokosten*
postcard *die Postkarte*
potato *die Kartoffel*
potato chips *die Chips (m pl)*
poultry *das Geflügel*
pound *das Pfund*
pour (verb) *gießen*
powder *das Waschpulver*
power *der Strom*
power outage *der Stromausfall*
prefer (verb) *vorziehen*
pregnancy test *der Schwangerschaftstest*

pregnant *schwanger*
prescription *das Rezept*
present *das Geschenk*
press *die Presse*
price *der Preis*
price list *die Preisliste*
print (photo) *der Abzug*
print (verb) *drucken*
produce seller
  der Gemüsehändler
proud *stolz*
prove (verb) *gehen lassen*
province *die Provinz*
public holiday *der Feiertag*
pump *die Pumpe*
purple *lila*
push (verb) *drücken*
put (verb) *stellen*

Q

quarter *das Viertel*
quick *schnell*
quite *ganz*
quite *ziemlich*

R

rabbit *das Kaninchen*
race *das Rennen*
racecourse *die Rennbahn*
rack *das Gestell*
radiator *der Heizkörper*
radio *das Radio*
rail *die Schiene*
railroad *die Eisenbahn*
rain (verb) *regnen*
rain boots
  die Gummistiefel (m pl)
rain forest *der Regenwald*
rape *die Vergewaltigung*
rarely *selten*
rash *der Ausschlag*
raspberry *die Himbeere*
rat *die Ratte*

raw *roh*
razor *das Rasiermesser*
read (verb) *lesen*
ready *fertig*
real estate office
  der Immobilienmakler
really *wirklich*
reboot (verb) *neu starten*
receipt *die Quittung*
receive (verb) *erhalten*
reception *der Empfang*
receptionist *die Empfangsdame/*
  der Empfangschef
reclaim tag *das Gepäcketikett*
recommend (verb) *empfehlen*
record *der Rekord*
record store *das*
  Plattengeschäft
recycling bin *der*
  Recyclingbehälter
red *rot*
reduction *die Ermäßigung*
refrigerator *der Kühlschrank*
region *die Region*
registration number *die*
  Zulassungsnummer
relatives *die Verwandten*
release (verb) *loslassen*
remote control *die*
  Fernbedienung
rent (verb) *mieten*
repair (verb) *reparieren*
replace (verb) *ersetzen*
report (verb) *berichten*
research *die Forschung*
reservation *die Reservierung*
reserve (verb) *reservieren*
rest *das Pausenzeichen*
restaurant *das Restaurant*
restrooms *die Toilette*
resuscitation *die*
  Wiederbelebung
retired *pensioniert*

return *der Return*
return ticket *die Rückfahrkarte*
reverse (verb) *rückwärts fahren*
rewind *der Rücklauf*
rib *die Rippe*
rice *der Reis*
right (correct) *richtig*
right (direction) *rechts*
ring *der Ring*
rinse (verb) *spülen*
ripe *reif*
river *der Fluss*
road *die Straße*
road signs *die Verkehrsschilder (n pl)*
roads *die Straßen (n pl)*
roadwork *die Straßenarbeiten (n pl)*
roast *der Braten*
robbery *der Raub*
robe *die Robe*
rock climbing *das Klettern*
rocks *Felsen (m pl)*
roll (film) *die Rolle*
roof *das Dach*
roofrack *der Dachgepäckträger*
roof tile *der Dachziegel*
room *das Zimmer*
room key *der Zimmerschlüssel*
root *die Zahnwurzel*
rope *das Seil*
rough *das Rough*
round *rund*
router *die Oberfräse*
row *die Reihe*
rowing machine *die Rudermaschine*
ruby *der Rubin*

rug *der Teppich*
run *der Lauf*
rush *die Binse*

S

sad *traurig*
safari park *der Safaripark*
safe *sicher*
safety measures *Sicherheitsvorkehrungen (f pl)*
sailing *das Segeln*
sailing boat *das Segelboot*
salad *der Salat*
salami *die Salami*
sales assistant *Verkäufer(in) (m f)*
salmon *der Lachs*
salt *das Salz*
salted *gesalzen*
same *gleich*
sand *der Sand*
sandal *die Sandale*
sandwich *das Sandwich*
sanitary napkin *die Damenbinde*
satellite navigation *das GPS-System*
satellite TV *das Satellitenfernsehen*
satnav *das Navi*
Saturday *der Samstag*
sauce *die Soße*
saucepan *der Kochtopf*
saucer *die Untertasse*
sauna *die Sauna*
sausage *die Wurst*
sauté (verb) *anbraten*
save (verb) *halten*
savings account *das Sparkonto*
savory *deftig*
say (verb) *sagen*
scale *die Personenwaage*

scan *der Scanner*
scared *erschrocken*
scarf *der Schal*
school *die Schule*
scissors *die Schere*
scoop *die Kugel*
scooter *der Roller*
score *die Noten*
screen romance *der Liebesfilm*
scuba diving *das Tauchen*
sea *das Meer*
seafood *die Meeresfrüchte (f pl)*
search (verb) *suchen*
season *die Jahreszeit*
seasons *die Jahreszeiten (f pl)*
seat *der Sitz*
seat belt *der Sicherheitsgurt*
second *zweiter*
second (time) *die Sekunde*
second floor *die erste Etage*
sedan *die Limousine*
see (verb) *sehen*
seedless *kernlos*
seeds *die Samen*
sell (verb) *verkaufen*
sell-by date *das Verfalldatum*
send (verb) *senden*
send off *der Platzverweis*
senior citizen *Senior(in) (m/f)*
sensitive *empfindlich*
sentence *das Strafmaß*
separately *getrennt*
September *der September*
serious *ernst*
serve *der Aufschlag*
serve (verb) *servieren*
server *der Ober*
services *die Dienstleistungen (f pl)*
set *das Bühnenbild*
seven *sieben*
sew (verb) *nähen*
shampoo *das Shampoo*
shark *der Hai*

sharp (mus.) *das Kreuz*
shaving foam *der Rasierschaum*
she *sie*
sheet *das Bettlaken*
shelf *das Warenregal*
sherbet *das Sorbet*
shirt *das Hemd*
shock *der Schock*
shoe *der Schuh*
shoe store *das Schuhgeschäft*
shoes *die Schuhe (m pl)*
shopping mall
  das Einkaufszentrum
short *kurz*
shorts *die Shorts (m pl)*
shoulder *die Schulter*
shout (verb) *schreien*
shower *die Dusche*
shower gel *das Duschgel*
shy *schüchtern*
sick *krank*
sickness *die Krankheit*
side *die Seite*
side-by-side refrigerator *der Gefrier-Kühlschrank*
side effect *die Nebenwirkung*
side order *die Beilage*
sidewalk *der Bürgersteig*
sightseeing *die Besichtigungstour*
sign *das Schild*
sign (verb) *unterschreiben*
signal *das Signal*
signature *die Unterschrift*
signpost *der Wegweiser*
silk *die Seide*
silver *das Silber*
singer *Sänger(in) (m/f)*
single bed *das Einzelbett*
single room *das Einzelzimmer*
sink *das Waschbecken*
siren *die Sirene*
sister *die Schwester*
six *sechs*

size *die Größe*
skate *der Schlittschuh*
sketch *die Skizze*
ski *der Wasserski*
ski (verb) *skifahren*
ski boots *die Skistiefel (m pl)*
ski poles *die Skistöcke (m pl)*
ski slope *der Skihang*
skiing *der Skisport*
skin *die Haut*
skirt *der Rock*
skis *die Skier (m pl)*
sleeping *das Schlafen*
sleeping bag *der Schlafsack*
sleeping berth *der Liegeplatz*
sleeping pill *die Schlaftablette*
slickers *die Regenbekleidung*
slide *die Rutsche*
slip *der Unterrock*
slip road *die Zufahrtsstraße*
slippers *die Hausschuhe (m pl)*
slope *der Hang*
slow *langsam*
slow down *Langsam fahren!*
small *klein*
smartphone *das Smartphone*
smash *der Schmetterball*
smile *das Lächeln*
smoke *der Rauch*
smoke (verb) *rauchen*
smoke alarm *der Rauchmelder*
smoking area *der Raucherbereich*
snack *der Snack*
snack bar *die Snackbar*
snake *die Schlange*
sneakers *die Turnschuhe (m pl)*
sneeze *das Niesen*
sneeze (verb) *nießen*
snore (verb) *schnarchen*
snorkel *der Schnorchel*
snow *der Schnee*

snow (verb) *schneien*
snowboard *das Snowboard*
snowboarding *das Snowboarden*
so *so*
soak (verb) *einweichen*
soap *die Seife*
soccer/soccer ball *der Fußball*
socks *die Socken (f pl)*
soda water *das Sodawasser*
sofa *das Sofa*
sofa bed *die Bettcouch*
soft *weich*
soft drinks *die alkoholfreien Getränke (n pl)*
soil *der Boden*
some *einige*
somebody *jemand*
something *etwas*
sometimes *manchmal*
son *der Sohn*
song *das Lied*
soon *bald*
sorry! *Entschuldigung!*
soup *die Suppe*
sour *sauer*
south *der Süden*
souvenir *das Souvenir*
souvenirs *die Andenken (n pl)*
spare tire *der Ersatzreifen*
speak (verb) *sprechen*
speaker *Sprecher(in) (m/f)*
specialty *die Spezialität*
specials *die Spezialitäten (f pl)*
speed limit *die Geschwindigkeitsbegrenzung*
speedometer *der Tachometer*
spices *die Gewürze (n pl)*
spider *die Spinne*
spinach *der Spinat*
spine *die Wirbelsäule*
splint *die Schiene*
splinter *der Splitter*
spoke *die Speiche*

sponge *der Schwamm*
spoon *der Löffel*
sport *der Sport*
sports center *das Sportzentrum*
sports goods *die*
    Sportartikel (m pl)
sprain *die Verstauchung*
spray *das Spray*
spring *der Frühling*
square *das Quadrat*
square (in town) *der Platz*
staff *das Personal*
stage *die Bühne*
stairs *die Treppe*
stalls *das Parkett*
stamp *die Briefmarke*
stand *der Ständer*
start (verb) *starten*
statement *die Aussage*
statue *die Statue*
stay (verb) *bleiben*
steak *das Steak*
steamed *gedämpft*
steering wheel *das Lenkrad*
step machine *der Stepper*
sterling *das Pfund-Sterling*
stew *der Eintopf*
stick *der Schläger*
sting *der Stachel*
stir (verb) *rühren*
stir-fry *das Pfannengericht*
stolen *gestohlen*
stomach *der Magen*
stomach ache *die*
    Magenschmerzen
stop *der Stop*
stop (verb) *anhalten*
stop! *halt!*
store *das Geschäft*
store assistant
    Verkäufer(in) (m/f)
stormy *stürmisch*
straight *gerade*

straight on *geradeaus*
strap *der Träger*
strawberry *die Erdbeere*
street map *der Stadtplan; die*
    Straßenkarte
street sign *das Straßenschild*
stress *der Stress*
string *die Schnur*
strong *stark*
student *Student(in) (m/f)*
student card *der Studentenausweis*
study *das Arbeitszimmer*
stuffed animal *das Kuscheltier*
suburb *die Vorstadt*
subway *die U-Bahn*
subway map *der U-Bahnplan*
subway station
    die U-Bahnstation
suit *der Anzug*
suitcase *der Koffer*
summer *der Sommer*
sun *die Sonne*
sunbathe (verb) *sonnenbaden*
sunbed *die Sonnenbank*
sunblock *der Sonnenblocker*
sunburn *der Sonnenbrand*
Sunday *der Sonntag*
sunflower oil *das Sonnenblumenöl*
sunglasses *die Sonnenbrille*
sunhat *der Sonnenhut*
sun lounger *die Sonnenliege*
sunny *sonnig*
sunrise *der Sonnenaufgang*
sunscreen *das Sonnenschutzmittel*
sunset *der Sonnenuntergang*
sunshine *der Sonnenschein*
suntan lotion *die Sonnenlotion*
supermarket *der Supermarkt*
support *die Stütze*
suppositories *das Zäpfchen*
surf *die Brandung*
surf (verb) *surfen*
surfboard *das Surfboard*

surgeon *der Chirurg*
surgery *das Sprechzimmer*
surprised *überrascht*
sweater *der Pullover*
sweatshirt *das Sweatshirt*
sweep (verb) *fegen*
sweet *süß*
sweet potato *die Süßkartoffel*
swim (verb) *schwimmen*
swimming *das Schwimmen*
swimming goggles
  die Schwimmbrille
swimming pool *das Schwimmbad*
swimsuit *der Badeanzug*
swing *die Schaukel*
switch *der Schalter*

T

table *der Tisch*
tablet *die Tablette*
tailor *der Schneider*
take (verb) *nehmen*
take off (verb) *starten*
talk (verb) *sprechen*
tall *groß*
tampon *der Tampon*
tan *die Sonnenbräune*
tank *der Kessel*
tax *die Steuer*
taxi *das Taxi*
taxi driver *der Taxifahrer*
taxi stand *der Taxistand*
tea *der Tee*
teabag *der Teebeutel*
team *das Team*
teapot *die Teekanne*
teaspoon *der Teelöffel*
teeth *die Zähne (m pl)*
telephone *das Telefon*
telephone box *die Telefonzelle*
television *das Fernsehen*
temperature *die Temperatur*
tennis *das Tennis*

tennis ball *der Tennisball*
tennis court *der Tennisplatz*
tennis racket *der Tennisschläger*
tent *das Zelt*
terminal *das Terminal*
text (SMS) *die SMS*
thank (verb) *danken*
thank you *Danke*
that/this *dieser(e) (m/f)*
the *der(m); die(f); das(n)*
theater *das Theater*
their *ihr(e)*
then *dann*
there *dort*
there is/are *es gibt*
thermometer *das Thermometer*
thermostat *der Thermostat*
thick *dick*
thick fog *der dichte Nebel*
thief *der Dieb*
thin *dünn*
think (verb) *denken*
third floor *die zweite Etage* **thirty**
  dreißig
three *drei*
throat *Kehle(f)*
throat lozenge *die Halspastille*
through *durch*
throw *der Wurf*
thumb *der Daumen*
Thursday *der Donnerstag*
ticket *der Fahrschein*
ticket gates *die Eingangssperre*
ticket inspector
  Schaffner(in) (m/f)
ticket office *der Fahrkartenschalter*
tie *die Krawatte*
tight *eng*
time *die Zeit*
timetable *der Fahrplan*
tip *die Spitze*
tissue *das Papiertaschentuch*
to *nach; zu; zum*

toast *der Toast*
toaster *der Toaster*
tobacco *der Tabak*
tobacconist
  Tabakwarenhändler(in) (m/f)
today *heute*
toe *die Zehe*
toilet paper *die Rolle*
  Toilettenpapier
toiletries *die Toilettenartikel (m pl)*
toll *die Maut*
tomato *die Tomate*
tomato ketchup
  das Tomatenketchup
tomorrow *morgen*
tongue *die Zunge*
tonight *heute abend*
too; also *auch*
tooth *der Zahn*
toothache
  die Zahnschmerzen (m pl)
toothbrush *die Zahnbürste*
toothpaste *die Zahnpaste*
tour *die Rundreise*
tour bus *der Stadtrundfahrtbus*
tour guide *Reiseleiter(in) (m/f)*
tourist *Tourist(in) (m/f)*
tourist attraction *die*
  Touristenattraktion
tourist information
  die Touristeninformation
tourist information office
  das Fremdenverkehrsbüro
tow (verb) *abschleppen*
towards *zu*
towel *das Handtuch*
towels *die Handtücher (n pl)*
town *die Stadt*
town center *das Stadtzentrum*
town hall *das Rathaus*
toy *das Spielzeug*
track *das Gleis*
traffic *der Verkehr*

traffic circle *der*
  Kreisverkehr
traffic jam *der Stau*
traffic light *die Verkehrsampel*
traffic lights *die*
  Verkehrsampeln (f pl)
train *der Zug*
train station *der Bahnhof*
tram *die Straßenbahn*
transportation *der Transport*
trash *der Papierkorb*
trash can *der Mülleimer*
travel agent
  der Reisebürokaufmann/
  die Reisebürokauffrau
travel-sickness pills *die*
  Reisekrankheitstabletten (f pl)
traveler's check *der Reisescheck*
tray *das Tablett*
tree *der Baum*
trekking *das Trekken*
tripod *das Stativ*
trout *die Forelle*
trunk (car) *der Kofferraum*
try *der Versuch*
T-shirt *das T-Shirt*
tub *die Dose*
tube *die Tube*
Tuesday *der Dienstag*
tumble dryer *der Trockner*
tuna *der Thunfisch*
turn (verb) *umdrehen*
tweezers *die Pinzette*
twelve *zwölf*
twenty *zwanzig*
twin beds *zwei*
  Einzelbetten (n pl)
twin room *das*
  Zweibettzimmer
two *zwei*
tire *der Reifen*
tire pressure *der Reifendruck*

U

ugly *hässlich*
umbrella *der Schirm*
uncle *der Onkel*
under *unter*
underpass *die Unterführung*
undershirt *das Unterhemd*
understand (verb) *verstehen*
underwear *die Unterwäsche*
uniform *die Uniform*
United States *die Vereinigten Staaten (m pl)*
university *die Universität*
unleaded *bleifrei*
until *bis*
up *oben*
upset *aufgebracht*
urgent *dringend*
us *uns*
use (verb) *gebrauchen*
useful *nützlich*
usual; usually *gewöhnlich*

V

vacate (verb) *frei machen*
vacation *der Urlaub*
vacuum cleaner *der Staubsauger*
vacuum flask *die Thermosflasche*
validate (verb) *bestätigen*
valuables *die Wertgegenstände (m pl)*
value *Wert (m)*
vegetables *die Gemüse (n pl)*
vegetarian *Vegetarier(in) (m/f)*
veggie burger *der vegetarische Hamburger*
vehicle *das Fahrzeug*
Venetian blind *die Jalousie*
very *sehr*
veterinarian *der Tierarzt/die Tierärztin*
video game *das Videospiel*
view *der Blick*

village *das Dorf*
vinegar *der Essig*
vineyard *der Weinberg*
virus *der Virus*
visa *das Visum*
vision *die Sehkraft*
visit *der Besuch*
visitor *Besucher(in) (m/f)*
vitamins *die Vitamintabletten (f pl)*
voice message *die Sprachmitteilung*
volume *das Volumen*
vomit (verb) *sich übergeben*

W

wait *warten*
waiting room *das Wartezimmer*
waitress *die Kellnerin*
wake up (verb) *aufwachen*
wake-up call *der Weckruf*
walk *der Schritt*
wall *die Mauer*
wallet *die Brieftasche*
want *möchten; wollen*
ward *die Krankenstation*
warm *warm*
wash (verb) *spülen*
washing machine *die Waschmaschine*
wasp *die Wespe*
watch *die Armbanduhr*
watch (verb) *zusehen*
water *Wasser (n)*
water bottle *die Wasserflasche*
waterfall *der Wasserfall*
watermelon *die Wassermelone*
waterskiing *das Wasserskifahren*
watersports *der Wassersport*

water valve *der Absperrhahn*
wave *die Welle*
wax *die Enthaarung*
way *der Weg*
we *wir*
weak *schwach*
weather *das Wetter*
website *die Website*
wedding *die Hochzeit*
Wednesday *der Mittwoch*
week *die Woche*
weekend *das Wochenende*
weigh (verb) *wiegen*
weight *das Gewicht*
welcome *willkommen*
well (health) *gesund*
west *der Westen*
wet *nass*
wet wipe *das Reinigungstuch*
wetsuit *der Taucheranzug*
whale *der Wal*
what? *was?*
wheat *der Weizen*
wheel *das Rad*
wheelchair *der Rollstuhl*
wheelchair access *der Zugang für Rollstuhlfahrer*
wheelchair ramp *die Rollstuhlrampe*
when? *wann?*
where? *wo?*
which? *welcher?*
whisk *der Schneebesen*
whiskey *der Whisky*
white *weiß*
who? *wer?*
whole *ganz*
whole-wheat bread *das Graubrot*
why? *warum?*

Wi-Fi *WLAN*
wide *breit*
width *die Breite*
wife *die Ehefrau*
win (verb) *gewinnen*
wind *der Wind*
window *das Fenster*
window seat *der Fensterplatz*
windshield *die Windschutzscheibe*
windshield wipers *die Scheibenwischer (m pl)*
windsurfing *das Windsurfing*
windy *windig*
wine *der Wein*
wine glass *das Weinglas*
wine list *die Weinkarte*
winter *der Winter*
winter sports *der Wintersport*
wipe (verb) *wischen*
with *mit*
withdrawal *die Abhebung*
without *ohne*
witness (noun) *Zeuge/Zeugin (m/f)*
woman *die Frau*
wood *der Wald*
wool *die Wolle*
work *die Arbeit*
worried *besorgt*
worse *schlechter*
wrapping paper *das Geschenkpapier*
wrist *das Handgelenk*
wrist watch *die Armbanduhr*
write (verb) *schreiben*
wrong *falsch*

X, Y, Z

X-ray *die Röntgenaufnahme*
yacht *die Jacht*
year *das Jahr*
yellow *gelb*
yes *ja*
yesterday *gestern*
yoga *das Joga*
yogurt *der Joghurt*

you *du (singular informal); Sie (singular formal; plural)*
young *jung*
your *dein (singular informal); Ihr (singular formal; ihr (plural)*
zero *null*
zipper *der Reißverschluss*
zone *die Zone*
zoo *der Zoo*
zucchini *die Zucchini*

The gender of German nouns is shown by (m), (f), and (n) for masculine, feminine, and neuter singular nouns and (m pl), (f pl) and (n pl) for plural nouns. Some nouns, such as jobs, change endings according to gender. The masculine form is shown, followed by the feminine ending in parentheses.

A

à la carte *à la carte*
Abend (m) *evening*
Abendessen (n) *dinner*
Abendmenü (n)
  evening menu
Abfertigungsschalter (m)
  check-in desk
Abflug (m) *take off*
Abflughalle (f)
  departures hall
abheben *to withdraw*
Abhebung (f) *withdrawal*
Absatz (m) *heel (shoe)*
abschleppen *to tow*
Absperrhahn (m)
  water valve
Abteil (n) *compartment*
Abzug (m) *print (photo)*
acht *eight*
Achtung *caution*
Adapter (m) *adapter*
addieren *to add*
Adresse (f) *address*
Aerobic (n) *aerobics*
Affe (m) *monkey*
After-Sun-Lotion (f)
  aftersun lotion
Airbag (m) *airbag*
Aktentasche (f) *briefcase*
Aktivitäten (f) *activities*
alkoholfreie Getränke (n pl)
  soft drinks

alkoholische Getränke (n pl)
  alcoholic beverages
Allee (f) *avenue*
allein *alone*
Allergie (f) *allergy*
allergisch *allergic*
alle(s) *all*
alt *old*
Amerikaner(in) (m/f)
  American
an *at; by*
an Bord gehen
  to board
anbraten *to sauté*
Andenken (n pl) *souvenirs*
andere *another*
  (different)
Anfang (m) *beginning*
Anfänger(in) (m/f)
  beginner
Angeln (n) *fishing*
Angelrute (f) *fishing rod*
angenehm *nice*
  (pleasant)
Angriff (m) *attack*
anhalten *to stop*
Anhang (m) *attachment*
Anklage (f) *charge*
ankommen *to arrive*
Ankunft (f) *arrivals*
Ankunftshalle (f)
  arrivals hall
Anorak (m) *parka*

Anprobe (f)
changing rooms
Anrufbeantworter (m)
answering machine
Antibiotika (n pl) *antibiotics*
Antiseptikum (n)
antiseptic
antworten *to answer*
Anwendung (f)
application
Anzahlung (f) *deposit*
Anzeige (f) *complaint*
Anzug (m) *suit*
Apfel (m) *apple*
Apfelsaft (m) *apple juice*
Apotheke (f) *pharmacy*
Apotheker(in) (m/f)
pharmacist
applaudieren *to applaud*
Aprikose (f) *apricot*
April (m) *April*
Arbeit (f) *work*
arbeiten *to work*
Arbeitszimmer (n) *study*
Architekt(in) (m/f) *architect*
Architektur (f) *architecture*
Arm (m) *arm*
Armband (n)
armband; bracelet
Armbanduhr (f) *watch*
Armlehne (f) *arm rest*
Arthrose (f) *arthritis*
Arzt (m) *doctor*
Arztpraxis (f)
doctor's surgery
Aschenbecher (m) *ashtray*
Assistentin (f) *assistant*
Ast (m) *branch*
Asthma (n) *asthma*
Aubergine (f) *eggplant*
auch *too; also*
Audioführer (m)
audio guide

auf *on; at*
Auf Wiedersehen!
goodbye
aufgeben *to mail*
aufgebracht *upset*
Auflösungszeichen (n)
natural
Aufschlag (m) *serve*
aufwachen *to wake up*
Auge (n) *eye*
Augenbraue (f) *eyebrow*
August (m) *August*
aus *from; off; out*
Ausflug (m) *excursion*
Ausflugsboot (n)
pleasure boat
Ausgang (m) *exit*
ausgehen *to go out*
ausländische Währung (f)
foreign currency
Ausleihe (f) *loan*
ausleihen *to borrow*
ausloggen *to log out*
Auspuff (m) *exhaust (car)*
Ausrüstung (f) *equipment*
Aussage (f) *statement*
ausscheiden *out*
Ausschlag (m) *rash*
Ausstellung (f) *exhibition*
äußere Erscheinung (f)
appearance
außerhalb *outside*
austauschen *exchange*
Australien *Australia*
Australier(in) (m/f)
Australian
auswärts essen *eating out*
Ausweis (m) *ID*
Auto (n) *car*
Autobahn (f) *highway*
Autoradio (n) *car stereo*
Autounfall (m) *car accident*
Autoverleih (m) *car rental*

Autovermietung (f)
car rental
Autowaschanlage (f) *car wash*
Avocado (f) *avocado*

B

Baby (n) *baby*
Babysitten (n)
babysitting
Backblech (n)
cookie sheet
backen *to bake*
Bäcker(in) (m/f) *baker*
Bäckerei (f) *baker*
Backofen (m) *oven*
Badeanzug (m)
swimsuit
Badekappe (f) *bathing cap*
Bademantel (m)
bath robe
Badetuch (n) *bath towel*
Badewanne (f) *bathtub*
Badezimmer (n) *bathroom*
Badminton (n) *badminton*
Bagel (m) *bagel*
Baguette (n) *baguette*
Bahnhof (m) *train station*
Bahnhofshalle (f)
concourse
Bahnsteig (m) *platform*
bald *soon*
Balkon (m) *balcony; gallery*
Ball (m) *ball*
Ballett (n) *ballet*
Banane (f) *banana*
Bank (f) *bench*
Bank (f) *bank*
Bankdirektor (m)
bank manager
Bankgebühr (f)
bank charge
Bankkonto (n)
bank account

Bar (f) *bar*
Bargeld (n) *cash*
Barkeeper (m) *bartender*
Bär (m) *bear*
Baseballhandschuh (m)
baseball glove
Basilikum (n) *basil*
Basketball (n)
basketball (game)
Batterie (f) *battery*
Bauarbeiter (m) *construction worker*
bauen *to build*
Bauernhof (m) *farm*
Baum (m) *tree*
Baumwolle (f) *cotton*
Baustelle (f) *construction site*
Becher (m) *mug*
beeilen *to hurry*
beenden *to finish*
Beere (f) *berry*
befestigen *to fix*
begeistert *excited*
beginnen *to begin*
behalten *to keep*
Behälter (m) *container*
Behinderte(r) (f/m)
disabled person
Behindertenparkplatz (m)
disabled parking
Beilage (f) *side dish*
Bein (n) *leg*
bekommen *to get*
beleuchten *to light*
Benzin (n) *gasoline*
Benzinuhr (f) *fuel gauge*
berechnen *to charge*
bereits *already*
Berg (m) *mountain*
Bericht (m) *report*
berichten *to report*
Berufe (m pl) *occupations*
beschädigt *damaged*

beschweren: sich beschweren
to complain
Besen (m) *broom*
besetzt *engaged/busy*
Besichtigungstour (f)
guided tour
besorgt *worried*
besser *better*
bestätigen *to validate*
Besteck (n) *cutlery*
bestellen *to order*
Bestellung (f) *order*
Besuch (m) *visit*
Besucher(in) (m/f) *visitor*
Betrag (m) *amount*
Bett (n) *bed*
Bettcouch (f) *sofa bed*
Bettdecke (f) *comforter*
Bettlaken (n) *sheet*
Bettwäsche (f) *bed linen*
bewölkt *cloudy*
bezahlen *to pay*
Bezirk (m) *district*
Bibliothek (f) *library*
Bidet (n) *bidet*
Biene (f) *bee*
Bier (n) *beer*
Bikini (m) *bikini*
billig *cheap*
Binse (f) *rush*
Birne (f) *pear*
bis *by; until*
Biss (m) *bite*
bitte *please*
bitter *bitter*
Blase (f) *blister*
blau *blue*
bleiben *to stay*
bleifrei *unleaded*
Bleistift (m) *pencil*
Blick (m) *view*
Blitzgerät (n) *flash gun*
Block (m) *block*

blond *blonde*
Blumen (f) *flowers*
Blumenarrangements (n pl)
flower arrangements
Blumenkohl (m)
cauliflower
Bluse (f) *blouse*
Blutdruck(m)
blood pressure
Blutprobe (f) *blood test*
Blutung (f) *bleeding*
Boden (m) *soil*
Bogen (m) *arc*
Bohnen (f) *beans*
Boje (f) *buoy*
Bonbons (m pl) *candy*
Bordkarte (f) *boarding pass*
Botschaft (f) *embassy*
Boutique (f) *boutique*
Bowling (n) *bowling*
Brand (m) *fire*
Brandung (f) *surf*
Braten (m) *roast*
Bratpfanne(f) *frying pan*
brauchen *to need*
braun *brown*
breit *wide*
Breitbildfernseher (m)
widescreen TV
Breite (f) *width*
Bremse (f) *brake*
Briefkasten (m) *mailbox*
Briefmarke (f) *stamp*
Brieftasche (f) *wallet*
Briefträger (m) *letter carrier*
Briefumschlag (m)
envelope
Brille (f) *glasses*
Brioche (f) *brioche*
britisch *British*
Brokkoli (m) *broccoli*
Brombeere (f) *blackberry*
Brot (n) *bread*

browsen *to browse*
Bruch (m) *fracture*
Bruder (m) *brother*
brünett *brunette*
Brust (f) *chest*
Buch (n) *book*
buchen *to book*
Buchladen (m)
  bookstore
Buffet (n) *buffet*
Bügelbrett (n)
  ironing board
Bügeleisen (n) *iron*
Bühne (f) *stage*
Bühnenbild (n) *set*
Bürgersteig (m)
  sidewalk
Büro (n) *office*
Bürste (f) *brush*
Bus (m) *bus*
Busbahnhof (m)
  bus station
Busfahrer(in) (m/f)
  bus driver
Bushaltestelle (f)
  bus stop
Büste (f) *bust*
Butter (f) *butter*
Butternusskürbis (m)
  butternut squash

C, D

Café (n) *café*
Cafetière (f) *French press*
Campingplatz (m) *campsite*
Cappuccino (m) *cappuccino*
CD (f) *CD*
CD-Spieler (m) *CD player*
Champagner (m) *champagne*
Check-in (m) *check-in*
Check-up (m) *checkup*
Chef (m) *manager*
Chips (m pl) *potato chips*

Chirurg (m) *surgeon*
Chorizo (f) *chorizo*
Cocktail (m) *cocktail*
Comic (m) *comic book*
Computer (m) *computer*
Couchtisch (m) *coffee table*
Cousin(e) (m/f) *cousin*
Crêpes (f) *crêpes*
Croissant (n) *croissant*
Curry (n) *curry*
Dach (n) *roof*
Dachgepäckträger (m)
  roofrack
Dachziegel (m) *roof tile*
Damenbinde (f)
  sanitary napkin
Danke *thank you*
danken *to thank*
dann *then*
das (n) *the*
Daumen (m) *thumb*
Decke (f) *ceiling*
Decke (f) *blanket*
Deckel (m) *lid*
dein *your*
Delfin (m) *dolphin*
Delikatessenladen (m)
  delicatessen
denken *to think*
Denkmal (n) *monument*
Deodorant (n) *deodorant*
der (m) *the*
Dessert (n) *dessert*
Dessertlöffel (m) *dessertspoon*
Dezember (m) *December*
Diabetiker(in) (m/f) *diabetic*
dichter Nebel (m) *thick fog*
dick *thick*
die (f) *the*
Dieb (m) *thief*
Dienstag (m) *Tuesday*
Dienstleistungen (f) *services*
diesel (m) *diesel*

dieser/e/es (m/f/n) *this*
Digitalkamera (f)
  digital camera
Digitalradio (n)
  digital radio
diskutieren *to discuss*
Disziplinen (f pl) *disciplines*
Dolmetscher(in) (m/f) *interpreter*
Dom (m) *cathedral*
Donnerstag (m) *Thursday*
Doppelbett (n) *double bed*
Doppelzimmer (n)
  double room
Dorf (n) *village*
dort *there*
Dose (f) *tub*
Dose (f) *can (noun)*
Dosenöffner (m)
  can opener
Dosierung (f) *dosage*
drechseln *to turn*
drei *three*
dringend *urgent*
drucken *to print*
drücken *push*
du *you*
dunkel *dark*
dünn *thin*
durch *through*
Durchfall (m) *diarrhea*
Dusche (f) *shower*
Duschgel (n) *shower gel*
Duty Free Store (m)
  duty-free shop
DVD (f) *DVD*
DVD-Player (m)
  DVD player

E

EC-Karte (f) *debit card*
Eckball (m) *corner*
Edelstein (m) *gem stone*
Ehefrau (f) *wife*

Ehemann (m) *husband*
Ei (n) *egg*
Eimer (m) *bucket*
ein wenig *a little*
einbrechen *to burgle*
einchecken *to check in*
einen Flug buchen
  to book a flight
Eingang (m) *entrance*
Eingangssperre (f)
  ticket gates
einige *some*
einkaufen gehen
  to go shopping
Einkaufszentrum (n)
  shopping mall
einloggen *to log on*
eins *one (number)*
Eintopf (m) *stew*
Eintrittskarte (f)
  entrance ticket
Einwanderung (f)
  immigration
einweichen *to soak*
einzahlen *to pay in*
ein Zelt aufschlagen
  to pitch a tent
Einzelbett (n) *single bed*
Einzelfahrt (f) *one-way ticket*
Einzelzimmer (n)
  single room
Einzugsauftrag (m)
  automatic payment
Eis (n) *ice*
Eisenbahn (f) *railroad*
eisig *icy*
Eislaufen (n) *ice-skating*
Elektriker (m) *electrician*
Ellbogen (m) *elbow*
Ellipsentrainer (m)
  cross trainer
Eltern (f) *parents*
E-Mail (f) *email*

emigrieren *to emigrate*
Empfang (m) *reception*
Empfängnisverhütung (f)
 contraception
Empfangsdame (f)
 receptionist
empfehlen *to recommend*
empfindlich *sensitive*
Ende (n) *end*
eng *tight*
Engländer(in) (m/f) *English*
Englisch *English (language)*
Entbindung (f) *delivery*
Ente (f) *duck*
Entfernung (f) *distance*
Enthaarung (f) *wax*
entlang *along*
Entschuldigung! *sorry!*
entwickeln
 to develop (film)
Epileptiker(in) (m/f)
 epileptic
er *he*
Erdbeben (n)
 earthquake
Erdbeere (f) *strawberry*
Erdnuss (f) *peanut*
Erdnussbutter (f)
 peanut butter
erhalten *to receive*
Erkältung (f) *cold*
Erlebnispark (m)
 amusement park
Ermäßigung (f)
 reduction
ernst *serious*
Ersatzreifen (m)
 spare tire
erschrocken *scared*
ersetzen *to replace*
erste *first*
erste Etage (f) *second floor*
Erste Hilfe (f) *first aid*

Erste-Hilfe-Kasten (m)
 first-aid box
ersticken *to choke*
Erwachsene (m/f) *adult*
es *it*
es gibt *there is/are*
Espresso (m) *espresso*
essen *to eat*
Essen (n) *food*
Essig (m) *vinegar*
Esszimmer (n) *dining room*
etwa *about; approximately*
etwas *something*
Euro (m) *euro*
Express-Service (m)
 express service
extra *extra*
Eyeliner (m) *eyeliner*

F

Fachbereich (m)
 department
Fahne (f) *flag*
Fähre (f) *ferry*
fahren *to drive*
Fahrer (m) *driver*
Fahrerkabine (f) *cab*
Fahrgeschäfte (n pl) *rides*
Fahrkartenschalter (m)
 ticket office
Fahrplan (m)
 timetable (train)
Fahrpreis (m) *fare*
Fahrrad (n) *bicycle*
Fahrradhelm (m)
 cycle helmet
Fahrradpumpe (f)
 bicycle pump
Fahrradschloss (n)
 cycle lock
Fahrradständer (m)
 bike rack
Fahrradweg (m) *cycle lane*

Fahrscheinautomat(m)
automatic ticket machine
Fahrschein (m) *ticket*
Fahrzeug (n) *vehicle*
falsch *wrong*
Familie (f) *family*
Familienkarte (f)
family ticket
Familienzimmer (n)
family room
fangen *to catch*
Farbe (f) *color*
Farbstift (m)
colored pencil
fast *almost*
Februar (m) *February*
fegen *to sweep*
Fehler (m) *mistake*
Feier (f) *celebration*
Feiertag (m)
bank holiday
Feld (n) *field*
Felsen (m pl) *rocks*
Fenster (n) *window*
Fensterplatz (m)
window seat
Fernbedienung (f)
remote control
Fernsehen (n) *television*
Fernsehkanal (m)
channel (TV)
Ferse (f) *heel*
fertig *ready*
Feste (n pl) *festivals*
festlegen *to fix*
Fett (n) *fat*
feucht *humid*
Feueralarm (m) *fire alarm*
Feuerlöscher (m)
fire extinguisher
Feuertreppe (f) *fire escape*
Feuerwehr (f) *fire department*
Feuerwehrauto (n) *fire engine*

Feuerwehrmann (m)
firefighter
Feuerzeug (n) *lighter*
Fieber (n) *fever*
Filet (n) *fillet*
Film (m) *movie*
Filmrolle (f) *roll of film*
finden *to find*
Finger (m) *finger*
Firma (f) *company*
Fisch (m) *fish*
Fischhändler(in) (m/f)
fish seller
Fitness (f) *fitness*
Fitness-Studio (n) *gym*
Fläche (f) *area*
Flasche (f) *bottle*
Flaschenöffner (m)
bottle opener
Flaschenwasser (n)
bottled water
Fleisch (n) *meat*
Fleischklöße (f) *meatballs*
fliegen *to fly*
Flip-Flops (f pl) *flip-flop*
Florist(in) (m/f) *florist*
Flossen (f pl) *flippers*
Flug (m) *flight*
Flugbegleiter(in) (m/f)
flight attendant
Flughafen (m) *airport*
Flugmahlzeit (f) *in-flight meal*
Flugnummer (f) *flight number*
Flugsteig (m) *boarding gate*
Flugverbindung (f) *flight
connection*
Flugzeug (n) *airplane*
Fluss (m) *river*
Flüssigreiniger (m) *liquid cleanser*
Föhn (m) *hairdryer*
föhnen *to blow dry*
Forelle (f) *trout*
Form (f) *form*

Forschung (f) *research*
Foto (n) *photograph*
Fotoalbum (n) *photo album*
Fotografie (f) *photography*
Fotografieren mit Blitzlicht (n)
  flash photography
Fotorahmen (m)
  photo frame
Frau (f) *woman*
frei *free*
Freibad (n) *outdoor pool*
Freigepäck (n)
  baggage allowance
Freitag (m) *Friday*
Freizeit (f) *leisure*
Fremdenverkehrsbüro (n)
  tourist information office
Freund(in) (m/f) *friend*
frisch *fresh*
Frisiersalon (m)
  hairdresser's
frittiert *deep-fried*
froh *happy*
Frost (m) *frost*
Frucht (f) *fruit*
früh *early*
Frühling (m) *spring*
Frühstück (n) *breakfast*
Frühstücksbuffet (n)
  breakfast buffet
Frühstücksspeck (m) *bacon*
Führer (m) *guide*
Führerschein (m)
  driving license
füllen *to fill*
Fundamt (n)
  lost property
fünf *five*
für *for*
furchtbar *awful*
Fuß (m) *foot*
Fußball (m) *soccer*
Fußboden (m) *floor*

Fußgängerübergang (m)
  pedestrian crossing
Fußrücken (m) *bridge*
Fußweg (m) *footpath*
Futteral (n) *case*

G

Gabel (f) *fork*
Gänge (m/pl) *courses*
Gang (m) *aisle*
Gangplatz (m)
  aisle seat
ganz *quite*
Garantie (f) *guarantee*
Garten (m) *garden*
Gas (n) *gas*
Gaskocher (m)
  camping stove
Gast (m) *guest*
Gastgeber (m) *host*
Gebäck (n) *pastry*
geben *to give*
Gebiss (n) *bit, set of teeth*
gebraten *fried*
gebrauchen *to use*
Gebrauchsanweisung (f)
  instructions
gebrochen *broken*
Geburt (f) *birth*
Geburtstag (m) *birthday*
Geburtsurkunde (f) *birth
  certificate*
gedämpft *steamed*
Geflügel (n) *poultry*
Gefrier-Kühlschrank (m)
  side-by-side refrigerator
gegenüber *opposite*
Geheimzahl (f)
  PIN
gehen *to go*
gehen lassen *to prove*
Gehirn (n) *brain*
gelangweilt *bored*

gelb *yellow*
Geld (n) *money*
Geldautomat (m)
 cash machine
Geldbeutel (m) *change purse*
gemahlen *ground*
Gemälde (n) *painting*
gemischt *mixed*
Gemüse (n pl) *vegetables*
Gemüsehändler (m)
 greengrocer
genau *exactly*
genießen *to enjoy*
Gepäckablage (f)
 luggage rack
Gepäckausgabe (f)
 baggage claim
Gepäcketikett (n)
 reclaim tag
Gepäck (n) *luggage*
Gepäckfach (n)
 overhead bin
Gepäcksaufbewahrung (f)
 left luggage
Gepäckträger (m) *porter*
gerade *straight*
geradeaus *straight on*
gesalzen *salted*
Geschäft (n) *business*
Geschäft (n) *store*
geschehen *to happen*
Geschenkboutique (f)
 gift store
Geschenk (n) *gift*
Geschenkpapier (n)
 wrapping paper
geschieden *divorced*
geschlossen *closed*
Geschwindigkeitsbegrenzung (f)
 speed limit
Gesicht (n) *face*
Gespräch (m) *phone call*
Gestänge (n) *frame*

Gestell (n) *rack*
gestern *yesterday*
gestohlen *stolen*
gesund *well (health)*
Gesundheit (f) *health*
Getränk (n) *drink (noun)*
Getränke (n pl) *drinks*
Getreideflocken (f) *cereal*
getrennt *separately*
Gewicht (n) *weight*
gewinnen *to win*
gewöhnlich *usual; usually*
Gewölbe (n) *arch*
Gewürze (n pl) *spices*
gießen *to pour*
Gin (m) *gin*
Giraffe (f) *giraffe*
Girokonto (n)
 checking account
Glanz (m) *gloss*
Glas (n) *glass*
gleich *same*
Gleis (n) *track*
Glühbirne (f) *light bulb*
Gold (n) *gold*
Golfball (m) *golf ball*
Golfclub (m) *golf club*
Golfplatz (m) *golf course*
Golfspiel (n) *golf*
Golf-Tee (n) *golf tee*
GPS-System (n)
 satellite navigation
Grade (m pl) *degrees*
Gramm (n) *gram*
grau *grey*
Graubrot (n) *whole-wheat bread*
Griff (m) *handle*
Grill (m) *barbecue*
grillen *to broil*
Grillpfanne (f) *griddle pan*
Grippe (f) *the flu*
groß *big; large*
Großbritannien *Great Britain*

Größe (f) *size*
(Groß)stadt (f) *city*
grün *green*
Grüntee (m) *green tea*
Gruppe (f) *group*
Gummistiefel (m pl)
rain boots
Gurke (f) *cucumber*
Gürtel (m) *belt*
Gürtelschnalle (f) *buckle*
gut *good; well*
Guten Abend! *Good evening*
Gute Nacht! *Good night*
Guten Morgen *Good morning*
Guten Tag *Good day*

H

Haar (n) *hair*
Haarbürste (f) *hair brush*
Haarfarben (f pl) *hair colors*
haben *to have*
Hackbrett (n)
cutting board
Hafen (m) *harbor*
Hafer (m) *oats*
Haferbrei (m) *porridge*
Hagel (m) *hail*
Hähnchen (n) *chicken*
Hai (m) *shark*
Hälfte (f) *half*
Hallenbad (n)
indoor pool
Hallo! *hello*
Halskette (f) *necklace*
Halspastille (f)
throat lozenge
halten *to hold*
Haltestelle (f) *bus stop*
Hamburger (m) *burger*
Hand (f) *hand*
Handbesen (m) *hand brush*
Handbuch (n) *manual*
Handgelenk (n) *wrist*

Handgepäck (n) *hand luggage*
Handschuhe (m pl) *gloves*
Handtasche (f) *handbag*
Handtücher (n pl) *towels*
Handtuch (n) *towel*
Handy (n) *cell phone*
Hang (m) *slope*
hart *hard*
hassen *to hate*
hässlich *ugly*
Hauptgericht (n)
main course
Hauptstadt (f) *capital*
Haus (n) *house*
Haushaltswarengeschäft (n)
hardware store
Hausschuhe (m pl) *slippers*
Haustier (n) *pet*
Haustür (f) *front door*
Haut (f) *skin*
Hecktürmodell (n) *hatchback*
Heidelbeere (f) *blueberry*
Heim (n) *home*
Heimtrainer (m) *exercise bike*
heiß *hot*
heiße Getränke (n pl)
hot drinks
heiße Schokolade (f)
hot chocolate
Heizkörper (m)
heater; radiator
Heizung (f) *heating*
helfen *to help*
hell *light (adj)*
Hemd (n) *shirt*
Herbst (m) *fall*
Hering (m) *tent peg*
Herrenfriseur (m) *barber*
herunterladen
to download
Herz (n) *heart*
Herzkrankheit (f)
heart condition

Heuschnupfen (m) *hay fever*
heute *today*
heute abend *tonight*
hier *here*
hier essen *eat-in*
Hilfe *help*
Himbeere (f) *raspberry*
hinter *behind*
hinunter *down*
Hobel (m) *plane*
Hochgeschwindigkeitszug (m)
  high-speed train
Hochschule (f) *college*
Hochzeit (f) *wedding*
Hockey (n) *hockey*
Hof (m) *courtyard*
Höhe (f) *height*
hoher Blutdruck (m)
  high blood pressure
Höhle (f) *cave*
Holzhammer (m) *mallet*
hören *to hear*
Hose (f) *pants*
Hotel (n) *hotel*
Hovercraft (n) *hovercraft*
hübsch *nice (attractive)*
Hüfte (f) *hip*
Hügel (m) *hill*
Hund (m) *dog*
Hupe (f) *horn (car)*
Hurrikan (m) *hurricane*
Husten (m) *cough*
Hustenmedikament (n)
  cough medicine
Hut (m) *hat*
Hydrant (m) *hydrant*

I

ich *I*
ihm, ihn *him*
Ihr *your*
ihr(e) *her; their*
immer *always*

Immobilienmakler (m)
  real estate office
in *at; in*
in Ohnmacht fallen
  to faint
Infektion (f) *infection*
Ingwer (m) *ginger*
Inhalator (m) *inhaler*
Inhalt (m) *contents*
innerhalb *inside*
Insektenschutzmittel (n)
  insect repellent
Insel (f) *island*
Intensivstation (f)
  intensive care unit
interessant *interesting*
Interesse (n) *interest*
Internet (n) *internet*
Internetcafé (n)
  internet café
Inventar (n) *inventory*
iPod (m) *iPod*
irgendeine (r) *anyone*
irgendetwas *anything*
Italien *Italy*
italienisch *Italian*

J

ja *yes*
Jacht (f) *yacht*
Jachthafen (m) *marina*
Jacke (f) *jacket*
Jahr (n) *year*
Jahreszeit (f) *season*
Jahreszeiten (f) *seasons*
Jalousie (f) *venetian blind*
Januar (m) *January*
Jazzclub (m) *jazz club*
Jeans (f pl) *jeans*
jede *every*
jeder *each*
jemand *somebody*
jenseits *beyond*

Jetski (m) *jet ski*
Jetskifahren (n) *jet skiing*
jetzt *now*
Joga (n) *yoga*
Jogging (n) *jogging*
Joghurt (m) *yogurt*
Juli (m) *July*
jung *young*
Junge (m) *boy*
Juni (m) *June*
Juwelier (m) *jeweler*

K

Kabel (n) *cable*
Kabelfernsehen (n) *cable television*
Kabeljau (m) *cod*
Käfer (m) *beetle*
Kaffee (m) *coffee*
Kaffeemaschine (f) *coffee machine*
Kaffeetasse (f) *coffee cup*
Kajak (n) *kayak*
Kalender (m) *calendar*
kalt *cold (adj)*
Kamera (f) *camera*
Kameratasche (f) *camera bag*
Kamm (m) *comb*
kampieren *to camp*
Kanada *Canada*
Kanal (m) *drain*
Kaninchen (n) *rabbit*
Kanu (n) *canoe*
Kapsel (f) *capsule*
Kapuze (f) *hood*
Karneval (m) *carnival*
Karotte (f) *carrot*
Karte (f) *card*
Karten (f pl) *cards*
Kartenspiel (n) *pack of cards*
Kartoffel (f) *potato*
Käse (m) *cheese*
Kasino (n) *casino*

Kasse (f) *box office*
Kasse (f) *cash register*
Kasse (f) *checkout*
Kassierer(in) (m/f) *checker*
Katze (f) *cat*
kaufen *to buy*
Kaufhaus (n) *department store*
Kaugummi (m) *chewing gum*
Kehle (f) *throat*
Kehrblech (n) *dustpan*
Keine Zufahrt! *No Entry!*
Keks (m) *cookie*
Kellergeschoss (n) *basement*
Kellnerin (f) *waitress*
kennen *to know (people)*
Kerngehäuse (n) *core*
kernlos *seedless*
Kessel (m) *tank*
Ketchup (m) *ketchup*
Kichererbsen (f pl) *chickpeas*
Kiefer (m) *jaw*
Kilo (n) *kilo*
Kilogramm (n) *kilogram*
Kilometer (m) *kilometer*
Kind (n) *child*
Kinder (n pl) *children*
Kinderbett (n) *crib*
Kindersitz (m) *child seat*
Kinderstuhl (m) *high chair*
Kinn (n) *chin*
Kino (n) *movie theater*
Kirche (f) *church*
Kirsche (f) *cherry*
Kirschtomate (f) *cherry tomato*
Klebestreifen (m) *adhesive tape*
Klebstoff (m) *glue*
Kleid (n) *dress*
Kleiderbügel (m) *coat hanger*

Kleiderschrank (m) *wardrobe*
Kleidung (f) *clothes*
klein *little*
Kleingeld (n) *change*
Klempner (in) (m/f) *plumber*
Klettern (n) *rock climbing*
Klient (m) *client*
Klimaanlage (f) *air-con*
Klingel (f) *bell*
Klinik (f) *clinic*
Klippe (f) *cliff*
Knabbereien (f pl) *bar snacks*
Knie (n) *knee*
Knoblauch (m) *garlic*
Knöchel (m) *ankle*
Knopf (m) *button*
kochen *to boil*
Kochen (n) *cooking*
Kochtopf (m) *saucepan*
Koffer (m) *suitcase*
Kofferkuli (m) *cart*
Kofferraum (m) *trunk (car)*
Kokosnuss (f) *coconut*
kommen *to come*
Kompass (m) *compass*
Kondom (n) *condom*
Konfitüre (f) *jam*
können *to be able to*
Konsul (m) *consul*
Konsulat (n) *consulate*
Konsultation (f) *consultation*
Kontaktlinsen (f pl) *contact lenses*
Kontinent (m) *continent*
Kontonummer (f)
  account number
Kontoüberziehung (f) *overdraft*
Konzert (n) *concert*
Kopf (m) *head*
Kopfhörer (m pl) *headphones*
Kopfkissen (n) *pillow*
Kopfschmerzen (f) *headache*
Kopfstütze (f) *head rest*

kopieren *to copy*
Korallenriff (n) *coral reef*
Korb (m) *basket*
Koriander (m) *cilantro*
Korken (m) *cork*
Korkenzieher (m)
  corkscrew
Körper (m) *body*
Körperlotion (f)
  body lotion
köstlich *delicious*
Kotelett (n) *chop*
Krabbe (f) *crab*
Krake (m) *octopus*
Krampf (m) *cramp*
krank *sick*
Krankenhaus (n) *hospital*
Krankenpfleger (m) *nurse*
Krankenschwester (f) *nurse*
Krankenstation (f)
  hospital ward
Krankenversicherung (f)
  health insurance
Krankenwagen (m)
  ambulance
Krankheit (f) *illness*
Kraut (n) *herb*
Krawatte (f) *tie*
Kreditkarte (f)
  credit card
Kreis (m) *circle*
Kreisverkehr (m)
  traffic circle
Kreuz (n) *club (games)*
Kreuz (n) *sharp (music)*
Krug (m) *pitcher*
Kruste (f) *crust*
Küche (f) *kitchen*
Küchenchef (m) *chef*
Küchenregal (n) *kitchen shelves*
Kugel (f) *scoop*
Kuh (f) *cow*
Kühlbox (f) *cooler*

Kühlschrank (m) *refrigerator*
Kunde (m) *customer*
Kunst (f) *art*
Künstlerin (f) *artist*
Kunstmuseum (n)
  art gallery
Kupplung (f) *gear shift*
Kurier (m) *courier*
Kurs (m) *course*
kurz *short*
kurzgebraten *pan fried*
Kuscheltier (n) *stuffed animal*
Küste (f) *coast*
Küstenwache (f) *coastguard*

L

Lächeln (n) *smile*
lachen *to laugh*
Lachs (m) *salmon*
Lamm (n) *lamb*
Land (n) *country*
Landwirt (m) *farmer*
lang *long*
Länge (f) *length*
langsam *slow*
Langsam fahren!
  Slow down!
Laptop (m) *laptop*
Lauf (m) *run*
laut *noisy*
Lebensgefahr (f) *danger*
Lebensmittel (n pl) *groceries*
Leck (n) *leak*
leer *empty*
Leerung (f) *collection*
legen *to put*
leger *casual*
Lehne (f) *back*
leicht *easy*
Leichtathlet(in) (m/f) *athlete*
leihen *to rent*
Lenkrad (n) *steering wheel*
lernen *to learn*

lesen *to read*
letzte *last*
letzte Woche *last week*
Leuchtturm (m) *lighthouse*
Licht (n) *light*
Lichtschalter (m)
  lights switch
lieben *to love*
Lied (n) *song*
Liegeplatz (m)
  mooring
Liegestuhl (m) *deck chair*
Lift (m) *elevator*
Liftpass (m) *lift pass*
lila *purple*
Limonade (f) *lemonade*
Limousine (f) *sedan*
Linde (f) *lime*
links *left*
Linse (f) *lens*
Liter (m) *liter*
lockig *curly*
Löffel (m) *spoon*
lokal *local*
loslassen *to release*
Luftpost (f) *airmail*

M

machen *to make*
Mädchen (n) *girl*
Magen (m) *stomach*
Magenschmerzen (m pl)
  stomach ache
Mahlzeit (f) *meal*
Mai (m) *May*
Mais (m) *corn*
Majonäse (f)
  mayonnaise
Make-up (n) *makeup*
manchmal *sometimes*
Mango (f) *mango*
Maniküre (f) *manicure*
Mann (m) *man*

Manschettenknöpfe (m pl)
    cufflinks
Mantel (m) *coat*
Manuskript (n) *manuscript*
Markt (m) *market*
März (m) *March*
Maschine (f) *machine*
Massage (f) *massage*
Maß (n) *measure*
Match (n) *match (sport)*
Matratze (f) *mattress*
matt *matte*
Mauer (f) *wall*
Maus (f) *mouse (computer)*
Maut (f) *toll*
Mechaniker(in) (m/f) *mechanic*
Medizin (f) *medicine*
Meer (n) *sea*
Meeresfrüchte (f) *seafood*
mehr *more*
Meile (f) *mile*
mein(e) *my*
Memory Card (f)
    memory card
Memory Stick (m)
    memory stick
Menschen (m pl) *people*
Messer (n) *knife*
Metall (n) *metal*
Meter (m) *meter*
Metzger (m) *butcher*
Mieder (n) *camisole*
mieten *to rent*
Migräne (f) *migraine*
Mikrowelle (f) *microwave*
Milch (f) *milk*
Milchprodukte (n pl) *dairy product*
Mineralwasser (n)
    mineral water
Minibar (f) *mini bar*
Minute (f) *minute*
Minze (f) *mint*
mit *with*

mit Automatik *automatic*
Mittag (m) *noon*
Mittagessen (n) *lunch*
Mittagsmenü (n)
    lunch menu
Mitte (f) *middle*
mittelgroß *medium*
Mittelstürmer (m) *forward*
Mitternacht (f) *midnight*
Mittwoch (m) *Wednesday*
Mixer (m) *blender*
Möbelgeschäft (n)
    furniture store
Mode (f) *fashion*
mögen *to want*
möglich *possible*
Monat (m) *month*
Montag (m) *Monday*
Mopp (m) *mop*
morgen *tomorrow*
Morgen (m) *morning*
Moskitonetz (n)
    mosquito net
Motor (m) *engine*
Motorrad (n) *motorcycle*
Mountainbike (n)
    mountain bike
Mozzarella (m)
    mozzarella
Muffin (m) *muffin*
Müll (m) *garbage*
Mülleimer (m)
    trash can
Mund (m) *mouth*
Mundwasser (n)
    mouthwash
Münze (f) *coin*
Münzfernsprecher (m)
    payphone
Museum (n) *museum*
Musik (f) *music*
Musiker(in) (m/f)
    musician

Muskeln (m pl) *muscles*
müssen *to have to*
Mutter (f) *mother*
Muttermal (n)
  mole (medical)
Mütze (f) *hood (car)*

N

nach *to*
nach *after*
Nachmittag (m) *afternoon*
Nachricht (f) *message*
Nachrichten (f pl) *news*
nächste *next*
nächste Woche *next week*
Nacht (f) *night*
Nachtclub (m) *nightclub*
Nachtisch (m) *dessert*
Nacken (m) *neck*
Nagel (m) *nail*
Nagelschere (f) *nail scissors*
Nagelzange (f) *nail clippers*
nah *close (near)*
nähen *to sew*
Name (m) *name*
Nascherei (f) *snack bar*
Nase (f) *nose*
Nasenbluten (n) *nosebleed*
nass *wet*
Nationalpark (m)
  national park
Naturreis (m) *brown rice*
Navi (n) *satnav*
navigieren *to navigate*
nebelig *misty*
neben *beside*
Nebenwirkung (f) *side effect*
nehmen *to take*
nein *no*
nervös *nervous*
Netz (n) *net*
Netzwerk (n) *network*
neu *new*

neu starten
  to reboot
neun *nine*
nicht *not*
nichts *nothing*
nie *never*
niederschlagen
  knock down
niedrig *low*
Niere (f) *kidney*
Niesen (n) *sneeze*
nießen *to sneeze*
noch ein(e) *another*
Norden (m) *north*
normal *normal*
Notaufnahme (f)
  emergency room
Notausgang (m)
  emergency exit
Notdienste (m pl)
  emergency services
Note (f) *bill (note)*
Noten (f) *score*
Notfall (m) *emergency*
Notizbuch (n) *notebook*
November (m) *November*
Nudeln (f) *pasta*
null *love*
null *zero*
Nummernschild (n)
  number plate
nur *only*
Nüsse (f pl) *nuts*
nützlich *useful*

O

oben *up*
Ober (m) *server*
Oberfräse (f) *router*
Obst (n) *fruit*
oder *or*
offen *open*
öffnen *to open*

Öffnungszeiten (f pl)
opening/ visiting hours
oft *often*
ohne *without*
Ohr (n) *ear*
Ohrring (m) *earring*
Okay *OK*
Oktober (m) *October*
Öl (n) *oil*
Oliven (f pl) *olives*
Olivenöl (n) *olive oil*
Omelett (n) *omelet*
Onkel (m) *uncle*
Online *online*
Oper (f) *opera*
Operation (f) *operation*
Opernhaus (n) *opera house*
orange *orange (color)*
Orangenmarmelade (f)
marmalade
Orangensaft (m)
orange juice
Ordnung: in Ordnung
alright; fine; OK
örtlich *local*
Osten (m) *east*
Ozean (m) *ocean*

P

Paar (n) *pair*
Paket (n) *packet; parcel*
Panne (f) *breakdown*
Papier (n) *paper*
Papiere (n pl) *papers (identity)*
Papierkorb (m) *trash*
Papiertaschentuch (n) *tissue*
Pappe (f) *cardboard*
Parfum (n) *perfume*
Park (m) *park*
Parkett (n) *stalls*
Parkplatz (m) *parking lot*
Parkuhr (f) *parking meter*
Parmesan (m) *parmesan*

Partner(in) (m/f)
partner
Pass (m) *passport*
Passagier(in) (m/f) *passenger*
Passkontrolle (f)
passport control
Pastete (f) *pie*
Patientenkurve (f) *patient curve*
Patient(in) (m/f) *patient*
Pause (f) *pause*
Pausenzeichen (n) *rest*
Pediküre (f) *pedicure*
pensioniert *retired*
Peperoni (f) *chilli pepper*
Personal (n) *staff*
Personenwaage (f) *scale*
Petersilie (f) *parsley*
Pfannengericht (n) *stir-fry*
Pfannkuchen (m pl) *crêpes*
Pfeffer (m) *pepper*
Pferd (n) *horse*
Pflanzen (f pl) *plants*
Pflanzenschildchen (n pl) *labels*
Pflaster (n) *adhesive bandage*
Pflaume (f) *plum*
Pflegespülung (f)
conditioner
Pfund (n) *pound*
Pfund-Sterling (n) *sterling*
Pianist(in) (m/f) *pianist*
Picknick (n) *picnic*
Picknickkorb (m)
picnic basket
Pilates (n) *pilates*
Pille (f) *pill*
Pilot(in) (m/f) *pilot*
Pilz (m) *mushroom*
PIN-Code (m) *PIN*
Pinnwand (f) *bulletin board*
Pint (n) *pint*
Pinzette (f) *tweezers*
Pizza (f) *pizza*
Planet (m) *planet*

Plattengeschäft (n)
  record store
Platz (m) *square (in town)*
Platzverweis (m) *send off*
Police (f) *policy*
Polizei (f) *police*
Polizeiwache (f) *police station*
Polizist(in) (m/f) *police officer*
Portion (f) *portion*
Portokosten (f) *postage*
Postamt (n) *post office*
Posteingang (m) *inbox*
Postkarte (f) *postcard*
Praline (f) *chocolate*
Preis (m) *price*
Preisliste (f) *price list*
Prellung (f) *bruise*
Presse (f) *press*
Programm (n) *program*
prost! *cheers!*
Provinz (f) *province*
Publikum (n) *audience*
Puderrouge (n) *blush*
Pullover (m) *sweater*
Pumpe (f) *pump*
Punkt (m) *point*
Puppe (f) *doll*
Putzfrau (f) *cleaner*

Q, R

Quadrat (n) *square*
Qualle (f) *jellyfish*
Quittung (f) *receipt*
Rad (n) *wheel*
Rad fahren *to cycle*
Radio (n) *radio*
Radiowecker (m)
  clock radio
Rahmkäse (m) *cream cheese*
Rasierapparat (m) *electric razor*
Rasiermesser (n) *razor*
Rasierschaum (m)
  shaving foam

Rathaus (n) *town hall*
Ratte (f) *rat*
Raub (m) *robbery*
rauben *to rob*
Rauch (m) *smoke*
rauchen *to smoke*
Raucherbereich (m)
  smoking area
Rauchmelder (m)
  smoke alarm
Raureif (m) *frost*
Rechnung (f) *check*
rechts *right (direction)*
Rechtsanwalt (m) /
  Rechtsanwältin (f) *lawyer*
Recyclingbehälter (m)
  recycling bin
Regenbekleidung (f)
  slickers
Regenwald (m)
  rain forest
Region (f) *region*
regnen *to rain*
Reibe (f) *grater*
reif *ripe*
Reifen (m) *tire*
Reifendruck (m) *tire pressure*
Reifenpanne (f) *flat tire*
Reihe (f) *row*
Reinigungsmittel (n) *cleaning
  material*
Reinigungstuch (n) *wet wipe*
Reis (m) *rice*
Reisebürokaufmann (m) /
  Reisebürokauffrau (f) *travel
  agent*
Reisebus (m) *coach*
Reiseführer (m) *guidebook*
Reisekrankheitstabletten (f)
  travel-sickness pills
Reiseleiter(in) (m/f)
  tour guide
reisen *to travel*

Reisescheck (m)
traveler's check
Reisetasche (f) *duffel bag*
Reiseziel (n) *destination*
Reißverschluss (m) *zipper*
Reiten (n) *horseback riding*
Rekord (m) *record*
Rennbahn (f) *racecourse*
Rennen (n) *race*
reparieren *to repair*
reservieren *to reserve*
Reservierung (f) *reservation*
Restaurant (n) *restaurant*
Rettungsring (m) *life ring*
Rettungsschwimmer(m)
lifeguard
Return (m) *return (sport)*
Rezept (n) *prescription*
Rezeption (f) *reception (hotel)*
richtig *right; correct*
Richtungsangaben (f pl) *directions*
Rindfleisch (n) *beef*
Ring (m) *ring*
Rippe (f) *rib*
Robe (f) *robe*
Rock (m) *skirt*
roh *raw*
Rolle Toilettenpapier (f)
toilet paper
Roller (m) *scooter*
Rollstuhl (m) *wheelchair*
Rollstuhlrampe (f)
wheelchair ramp
Röntgenaufnahme (f) *X-ray*
rosa *pink*
rot *red*
Rote Bete (f) *beet*
Rough (n) *rough (golf)*
Rubin (m) *ruby*
Rücken (m) *back (body)*
Rückfahrkarte (f) *return ticket*
Rücklauf (m) *rewind*
Rucksack (m) *backpack*

Rückseite (f) *back (not front of)*
rückwärts fahren *to reverse*
Ruder (n) *oar*
Rudermaschine (f)
rowing machine
Rufknopf (m) *call button*
Rufnummer (f) *contact number*
ruhig *calm*
rühren *to stir*
Rummelplatz (m) *fairground*
rund *round*
Rundreise (f) *tour*
Rutsche (f) *slide*

S

Safaripark (m) *safari park*
Saft (m) *juice*
sagen *to say; to tell*
Salami (f) *salami*
Salat (m) *salad*
Salbe (f) *ointment*
Salz (n) *salt*
salzig *salty*
Samen (m pl) *seeds*
Samstag (m) *Saturday*
Sand (m) *sand*
Sandale (f) *sandal*
Sandwich (n) *sandwich*
Sänger(in) (m/f) *singer*
Sanner (m) *scan*
Satellitenfernsehen (n)
satelliteTV
sauber *clean*
säubern *to clean*
sauer *sour*
Sauna (f) *sauna*
Schabe (f) *cockroach*
Schachtel (f) *box*
Schaffner(in) (m/f) *ticket inspector*
schälen *to peel*
Schal (m) *scarf*
Schäler (m) *peeler*
Schalter (m) *desk*

scharf *hot (spicy)*
schauen *to look*
Schaukel (f) *swing*
Schaumbad (n) *bubblebath*
Schauspieler(in) (m/f) *actor*
Scheck (m) *check*
Scheckbuch (n) *checkbook*
Scheckkarte (f) *check card*
Scheibenwischer (m pl)
 windshield wipers
Scheinwerfer (m) *headlight*
Schere (f) *scissors*
Schiene (f) *splint*
Schiff (n) *boat; ship*
Schifffahrt(f) *boat trip*
Schild (n) *sign*
Schirm (m) *umbrella*
Schlafanzug (m) *pajamas*
Schlafen (n) *sleeping*
Schlafsack (m) *sleeping bag*
Schlaftablette (f) *sleeping pill*
Schlafzimmer (n) *bedroom*
Schläger (m) *stick*
Schlange (f) *snake*
schlecht *bad*
schlechter *worse*
schließen *to close*
Schließfächer (n pl) *lockers*
Schlittschuh (m) *skate*
Schloss (n) *castle; lock*
Schlüssel (m) *key*
schmal *narrow*
Schmerz (m) *pain*
Schmerzmittel (n) *painkiller*
Schmetterball (m) *smash*
Schmuck (m) *jewelry*
schmutzig *dirty*
schnarchen *to snore*
Schnee (m) *snow*
Schneebesen (m) *whisk*
Schneider (m) *tailor*
schneien *to snow*
schnell *fast; quick*

Schnitt (m) *cut*
Schnorchel (m) *snorkel*
Schnupfen (m) *cold*
Schnur (f) *string*
Schock (m) *shock*
schön *beautiful*
schreiben *to write*
schreien *to shout*
Schritt (m) *walk*
Schublade (f) *drawer*
schüchtern *shy*
Schuh (m) *shoe*
Schuhe (m pl) *shoes*
Schuhgeschäft (n)
 shoe store
schulden *to owe*
Schule (f) *school*
Schulter (f) *shoulder*
Schürze (f) *apron*
Schüssel (f) *dish*
Schutzbrille (f) *goggles*
Schutzpolster (n) *pads*
schwach *weak*
Schwamm (m) *sponge*
schwanger *pregnant*
Schwangerschaftstest (m)
 pregnancy test
schwarz *black*
schwarze Johannisbeere (f)
 blackcurrant
schwarzer Kaffee (m)
 black coffee
schwarzetee (m) *black tea*
Schweinefleisch (n) *pork*
schwer *heavy*
Schwester (f) *sister*
schwierig *difficult*
Schwimmbad (n) *swimming pool*
Schwimmbrille (f)
 swimming goggles
Schwimmen (n) *swimming*
Schwimmkissen (n) *float*
Schwimmweste (f) *life jacket*

sechs *six*
See (m) *lake*
Segelboot (n) *sailing boat*
Segeln (n) *sailing*
sehen *to see*
Sehenswürdigkeiten (f pl)
    attractions
Sehkraft (f) *vision*
sehr *very*
Seide (f) *silk*
Seife (f) *soap*
Seil (n) *rope*
Seilbahn (f) *cable car*
Seite (f) *side*
Sekunde (f) *second*
selbst *myself*
selbstsicher *confident*
selten *rarely*
senden *to send*
Senf (m) *mustard*
Senior(in) (m/f) *senior citizen*
September (m) *September*
servieren *to serve*
Serviette (f) *napkin*
Sessellift (m) *chair lift*
setzen *to put*
Shampoo (n) *shampoo*
Shorts (m pl) *shorts*
sicher *safe*
Sicherheitsvorkehrungen (f)
    safety measures
sich übergeben *to vomit*
Sicherungskasten (m) *fuse box*
sie *she; they*
Sie *you*
Sieb (n) *colander*
sieben *seven*
Signal (n) *signal*
Silber (n) *silver*
Sirene (f) *siren*
Sitz (m) *seat*
sitzen *to sit*
Skier (m pl) *skis*

skifahren *to ski*
Skihang (m) *ski slope*
Skisport (m) *skiing*
Skistiefel (m pl) *ski boots*
Skistöcke (m pl) *ski poles*
Skizze (f) *sketch*
Slip (m) *briefs*
Smartphone (n) *smartphone*
SMS (f) *text (SMS)*
Snack (m) *snack*
Snackbar (f) *snack bar*
Snowboard (n) *snowboard*
Snowboarding (n)
    snowboarding
so *so*
Socken (f pl) *socks*
Sodawasser (n)
    soda water
Sofa (n) *sofa*
Sofakissen (n) *cushion*
Sohn (m) *son*
Sommer (m) *summer*
Sonne (f) *sun*
Sonnenaufgang (m) *sunrise*
sonnenbaden *to sunbathe*
Sonnenbank (f) *sunbed*
Sonnenblocker (m) *sunblock*
Sonnenblumenöl (n)
    sunflower oil
Sonnenbrand (m) *sunburn*
Sonnenbräune (f) *tan*
Sonnenbrille (f) *sunglasses*
Sonnenhut (m) *sunhat*
Sonnenliege (f) *lounge chair*
Sonnenlotion (f) *suntan lotion*
Sonnenschein (m) *sunshine*
Sonnenschirm (m)
    beach umbrella
Sonnenschutzmittel (n) *sunscreen*
Sonnenuntergang (m) *sunset*
sonnig *sunny*
Sonntag (m) *Sunday*
Sorbet (n) *sherbet*

Soße (f) *sauce*
Souvenir (n) *souvenir*
Spachtel (m) *spatula*
Sparkonto (n)
  savings account
spät *late*
Speiche (f) *spoke*
Speisewagen (m)
  dining car
Spezialität (f) *specialty*
Spezialitäten (f pl) *specialities*
Spiegel (m) *mirror*
Spiel (n) *match (sport)*
Spielbahn (f) *pitch*
spielen *to play (games)*
Spielmarke (f) *counter*
Spielplatz (m) *playground*
Spielzeug (n) *toy*
Spinat (m) *spinach*
Spinne (f) *spider*
Spitze (f) *tip*
Splitter (m) *splinter*
Sport (m) *sport*
Sportartikel (m pl) *sports goods*
Sportzentrum (n)
  sports center
Sprachmitteilung (f)
  voice message
Spray (n) *spray*
sprechen *to speak; to talk*
Sprecher(in) (m/f) *speaker*
Sprechzimmer (n) *surgery*
Springbrunnen (m) *fountain*
springen *to dive*
Spritze (f) *injection*
spülen *to rinse/ to wash*
Spülmaschine (f) *dishwasher*
Stachel (m) *sting*
Stadt (f) *town*
Stadtplan (m) *streetmap*
Stadtrundfahrtbus (m) *tour bus*
Stadtzentrum (n) *town center*
Ständer (m) *stand*

stark *strong*
starten *to start*
Stativ (n) *tripod*
Statue (f) *statue*
Stau (m) *traffic jam*
Steak (n) *steak*
Stechmücke (f) *mosquito*
Stecker (m) *plug*
stellen *to put*
Stepper (m) *step machine*
Steuer (f) *tax*
Stich (m) *engraving*
Stiefel (m) *boot*
Stoff (m) *fabric*
stolz *proud*
Stop (m) *stop*
Stoßstange (f) *bumper*
Strafe (f) *fine (legal)*
Strafmaß (n) *sentence*
Strand (m) *beach*
Strandball (m) *beach ball*
Straßen (f) *roads*
Straßenarbeiten (f pl) *roadwork*
Straßenbahn (f) *tram*
Straßenkarte (f) *street map*
Straßenschild (n) *street sign*
Strauß (m) *bunch*
Streichholz (n) *match (light)*
Streifenwagen (m) *police car*
Stress (m) *stress*
Strickjacke (f) *cardigan*
Stromausfall (m) *power outage*
Strom (m) *electricity*
Strumpfhose (f) *panty hose*
Stück (n) *piece; slice*
Studentenausweis (m)
  student card
Student(in) (m/f) *student*
Stuhl (m) *chair*
Stunde (f) *hour*
stürmisch *stormy*
Stütze (f) *support*
suchen *to search*

Süden (m) *south*
Supermarkt (m) *supermarket*
Suppe (f) *soup*
surfen *to surf*
süß *sweet*
Süßkartoffel (f) *sweet potato*
Süßstoff (m)
artificial sweetener
Sweatshirt (n) *sweatshirt*

T

Tabak (m) *tobacco*
Tabakwarenhändler(in) (m/f)
tobacconist
Tablett (n) *tray*
Tablette (f) *tablet; pill*
Tachometer (m) *speedometer*
Tag (m) *day*
Tampon (m) *tampon*
Tankstelle (f) *gas station*
Tante (f) *aunt*
Tanzen (n) *dancing*
Tanzmusik (f) *dance*
Tasche (f) *bag*
Taschenlampe (f) *flashlight*
Taschenrechner (m) *calculator*
Tasse (f) *cup*
Tastatur (f) *keyboard*
Tauchen (n) *diving*
Taucheranzug (m) *wetsuit*
Taxi (n) *taxi*
Taxifahrer(in) (m/f) *taxi driver*
Taxistand (m) *taxi stand*
Team (n) *team*
Tee (m) *tea*
Teebeutel (m) *teabag*
Teekanne (f) *teapot*
Teelöffel (m) *teaspoon*
Teilchen (n) *bun*
teilnehmen *to attend*
Telefonkarte (f) *phone card*
Telefonzelle (f) *telephone box*
Teller (m) *plate*

Temperatur (f) *temperature*
Tennis (n) *tennis*
Tennisball (m) *tennis ball*
Tennisplatz (m) *tennis court*
Tennisschläger (m)
tennis racket
Teppich (m) *carpet*
Termin (m) *appointment*
Terminal (n) *terminal*
Terminkalender (m) *day planner*
teuer *expensive*
Theater (n) *theater*
Theaterstück (n) *play*
Thermometer (n) *thermometer*
Thermosflasche (f) *vacuum flask*
Thermostat (m) *thermostat*
Thunfisch (m) *tuna*
tiefgefroren *frozen*
Tierärztin (f) *veterinarian*
Tiere (n pl) *animals*
Tisch (m) *table*
Toast (m) *toast*
Toaster (m) *toaster*
Tochter (f) *daughter*
Toilette (f) *restrooms*
Toilettenartikel (f) *toiletries*
Toilettenpapier (n)
toilet paper
Tomate (f) *tomato*
Tomatenketchup (n)
tomato ketchup
Töpferware (f) *dishes*
Tor (n) *gate*
Tourist(in) (m/f) *tourist*
Touristenattraktion (f)
tourist attraction
Touristeninformation (f)
tourist information
tragen *to carry*
Träger (m) *strap*
Tragflügelboot (n)
hydrofoil
traurig *sad*

Trekking (n) *trekking*
Treppe (f) *stairs*
trinken *to drink*
trocken *dry*
Trockner (m) *tumble dryer*
T-Shirt (n) *T-shirt*
Tube (f) *tube*
Tür (f) *door*
Türklingel (f) *doorbell*
Turnschuhe (m pl) *sneakers*
Tüte (f) *carton*

U

U-Bahn (f)
  subway
U-Bahnplan (m)
  subway map
U-Bahnstation (f)
  subway station
Übelkeit (f) *nausea*
über *over; across; more than*
überholen *to pass*
Übernachtung mit Frühstück (f)
  bed and breakfast
überrascht *surprised*
Überschwemmung (f) *flood*
Überweisung (f)
  bank transfer
Uhr (f) *clock; watch; o'clock*
um *around*
umdrehen *to turn*
Umkleidekabine (f)
  fitting room
umsteigen *to change*
und *and*
Unfall (m) *accident*
Unfallstation (f) *Accident and Emergency department*
Uniform (f) *uniform*
Universität (f) *university*
unmöglich *impossible*
uns *us*
unser *our*

unter *below*
Unterführung (f) *underpass*
unterhalb *beneath*
Unterhemd (n) *undershirt*
Unterkunft (f) *accommodation*
Unterrock (m) *slip*
unterschreiben *to sign*
Unterschrift (f) *signature*
Untersetzer (m) *coaster*
untersuchen *to examine*
Untersuchung (f) *examination*
Untertasse (f) *saucer*
Unterwäsche (f) *underwear*
Urlaub (m) *vacation*

V

Vater (m) *father*
Vegetarier(in) (m/f)
  vegetarian
vegetarische Hamburger (m)
  veggie burger
Ventilator (m) *fan*
Venusmuschel (f) *clam*
verärgert *angry*
Verband (m) *bandage; dressing*
Verbrechen (n) *crime*
Verbrennung (f) *burn (med.)*
Vereinigten Staaten (m pl)
  United States
Verfalldatum (n) *sell-by date*
Verfallsdatum (n)
  expiration date
vergessen *to forget*
Vergewaltigung (f) *rape*
verheiratet *married*
verkaufen *to sell*
Verkäufer(in) (m/f) *sales assistant*
Verkehr (m) *traffic*
Verkehrsampel (f) *traffic lights*
Verkehrsschilder (n pl) *road signs*
Verkehrsunfall (m) *car crash*
Verkühlung (f) *chill*
verlangen *to charge*

Verlängerungskabel (n) *extension lead*
verlassen *to leave*
verlegen *embarrassed*
verletzen *to injure*
Verletzung (f) *injury*
verlieren *to lose*
Versicherung (f) *insurance*
Versicherungsgesellschaft (f) *insurance company*
Versicherungspolice (f) *insurance policy*
verspätet *delayed*
Verstauchung (f) *sprain*
verstehen *to understand*
Verstopfung (f) *constipation*
Versuch (m) *try*
versuchen *to try*
Verwandten (f/m pl) *relatives*
verwirrt *confused*
Videospiel (n) *video game*
viel *a lot; much*
vielleicht *perhaps*
vier *four*
Viertel (n) *quarter*
Virus (m) *virus*
Visum (n) *visa*
Vitamintabletten (f pl) *vitamins*
Vögel (m pl) *birds*
voll *full*
Volumen (n) *volume*
von *from; of*
von Bord gehen *to disembark*
vor *before; in front of*
Vorhang (m) *curtain*
Vorspeise (f) *appetizer*
Vorstadt (f) *suburb*
vorziehen *to prefer*

W

Waagschale (f) *pan*
wählen *to dial*
während *during*

Wal (m) *whale*
Wald (m) *wood*
Wandern (n) *hiking*
Wanderschuhe (m pl) *hiking boots*
Wange (f) *cheek*
wann? *when?*
Warenregal (n) *shelf*
warm *warm*
Warnleuchten (f pl) *hazard lights*
warten *to wait*
Wartezimmer (n) *waiting room*
warum? *why?*
was? *what?*
Waschbecken (n) *sink*
Waschmaschine (f) *washing machine*
Waschpulver (n) *detergent*
Waschsalon (m) *laundromat*
Wasser (n) *water*
Wasserfall (m) *waterfall*
Wasserflasche (f) *water bottle*
Wasserhahn (m) *faucet*
Wasserkessel (m) *kettle*
Wassermelone (f) *watermelon*
Wasserskifahren (n) *waterskiing*
Wasserski (m) *ski*
Wassersport (m) *watersports*
Website (f) *website*
Wechselkurs (m) *exchange rate*
wechseln *to change*
Wechselstube (f) *currency exchange*
Wecker (m) *alarm clock*
Weckruf (m) *wake-up call*
Weg (m) *way*
Wegweiser (m) *signpost*
weich *soft*
Weinberg (m) *vineyard*
weinen *to cry*
Weinglas (n) *wine glass*
Weinkarte (f) *wine list*
weiß *white*

weit *far*
Weizen (m) *wheat*
welcher? *which?*
Welle (f) *wave*
wer? *who?*
Werkstatt (f) *garage*
Wertgegenstände (m pl)
  valuables
Wespe (f) *wasp*
Westen (m) *west*
Wetter (n) *weather*
Whisky (m) *whiskey*
Wickelraum (m) *baby
  changing room*
wie *as; how?*
wieder *again*
Wiederbelebung (f) *resuscitation*
wiegen *to weigh*
wie viel(e)? *how many?*
willkommen *welcome*
Wimper (f) *eyelash*
Wimperntusche (f) *mascara*
Windel (f) *diaper*
windig *windy*
Windschutzscheibe (f) *windshield*
Windsurfer(in) (m/f) *windsurfer*
Winter (m) *winter*
Wintersport (m) *winter sports*
wir *we; us*
Wirbelsäule (f) *spine*
wirklich *really*
wischen *to wipe*
wissen *to know (facts)*
WLAN *Wi-Fi*
wo? *where?*
Woche (f) *week*
Wochenende (n) *weekend*
Wohnblock (m) *apartment block*
Wohnung (f) *apartment*
Wohnwagen (m) *camper van*
Wohnwagenplatz (m) *camper van
  site*
Wohnzimmer (n) *living room*

Wolke (f) *cloud*
Wolle (f) *wool*
wollen *to want*
Wörterbuch (n) *dictionary*
Wurflinie (f) *crease*
Wurf (m) *throw*
Wurst (f) *sausage*
Wüste (f) *desert*

Z

Zahl (f) *number*
zahlen *to pay*
zählen *to count*
Zahlung (f) *payment*
Zahn (m) *tooth*
Zahnarzt (m) *dentist*
Zahnbürste (f) *toothbrush*
Zähne (m pl) *teeth*
Zahnpaste (f) *toothpaste*
Zahnschmerzen (m pl)
  toothache
Zahnwurzel (f) *root*
Zäpfchen (n) *suppository*
Zaun (m) *fence*
Zehe (f) *toe*
zeichnen *to draw*
Zeichnung (f) *drawing*
Zeit (f) *time*
Zeitschrift (f) *magazine*
Zeitung (f) *newspaper*
Zelt (n) *tent*
zelten *to camp*
Zentralheizung (f) *central heating*
Zentrum (n) *center*
zerbrechlich *fragile*
zerstoßen *crushed*
Ziegelstein (m) *brick*
ziemlich *quite*
Zigarre (f) *cigar*
Zigaretten (f pl) *cigarettes*
Zimmer (n) *room*
Zimmerschlüssel (m)
  room key

Zimt (m) *cinnamon*
Zitrone (f) *lemon*
Zitronengras (n)
  lemon grass
Zitrusfrüchte (f pl)
  citrus fruits
Zoll (m) *customs*
Zoll (m) *inch*
Zone (f) *zone*
Zoo (m) *zoo*
zu *to*
zu *towards*
Zucchini (f) *zucchini*
Zugang für Rollstuhlfahrer (m)
  wheelchair access
Zug (m) *move (game)*
Zug (m) *train*

zuhören *to listen*
zum; zur *to*
zum Mitnehmen
  carry out
Zunge (f) *tongue*
zusehen *to watch*
zwanzig *twenty*
zwei *two*
zwei Einzelbetten (n pl)
  twin beds
Zweibettzimmer (n) *room with*
  twin beds
zweite Etage (f) *third floor*
zweiter *second*
Zwiebel (f) *bulb*
Zwiebel (f) *onion*
zwischen *between*

ACKNOWLEDGMENTS

ORIGINAL EDITION

Senior Editors Simon Tuite, Angela Wilkes
Editorial Assistant Megan Jones
US Editor Margaret Parrish
Senior Art Editor Vicky Short
Art Editor Mandy Earey
Production Editor Phil Sergeant
Production Controller Inderjit Bhullar
Managing Editor Julie Oughton
Managing Art Editor Louise Dick
Art Director Bryn Walls
Associate Publisher Liz Wheeler
Publisher Jonathan Metcalf

Produced for Dorling Kindersley by SP Creative Design
Editor Heather Thomas
Designer Rolando Ugolino
Language content for Dorling Kindersley by First Edition Translations Ltd
Translator Ingrid Price-Gschlossl
Editor Tamara Benscheidt
Typesetting Essential Typesetting

Dorling Kindersley would also like to thank the following for their help in the preparation of the original and revised editions of this book: Isabelle Elkaim and Melanie Fitzgerald of First Edition Translations Ltd; Elma Aquino, Mandy Earey, and Meenal Goel for design assistance; Amelia Collins, Nicola Hodgson, Isha Sharma, Janashree Singha, Nishtha Kapil, and Neha Samuel for editorial assistance; Claire Bowers, Lucy Claxton, and Rose Horridge in the DK Picture Library; Adam Brackenbury, Vânia Cunha, Almudena Diaz, Maria Elia, John Goldsmid, Sonia Pati, Phil Sergeant, and Louise Waller for DTP assistance.

PICTURE CREDITS

The publisher would like to thank the following for their kind permission to reproduce their photographs:
Key: a (above); b (below/bottom); c (centre); l (left); r (right); t (top)
Alamy Images: Justin Kase p113 cb; Martin Lee p52 tr; PhotoSpin, Inc p38 crb;
Alamy Stock Photo: Cultura RM p51 br; **Courtesy of Renault:** p26–27 t; **Getty Images:** Bloomberg p4; Reggie Casagrande p148; **PunchStock:** Moodboard p8;
123RF.com: Cobalt p108 cr; Norman Kin Hang Chan / Bedo p109 cl; Cobalt p134 clb; Cobalt p156 br.

All other images © **Dorling Kindersley**
For further information, see: **www.dkimages.com**

NUMBERS

0 null *nool*	**6** sechs *zeks*	**12** zwölf *tsvurlf*	**18** achtzehn *akht-tsayn*	**60** sechzig *zekh-tsik*
1 eins *ines*	**7** sieben *zee-ben*	**13** dreizehn *dry-tsayn*	**19** neunzehn *noyn-tsayn*	**70** siebzig *zeep-tsik*
2 zwei *tsvy*	**8** acht *akht*	**14** vierzehn *feer-tsayn*	**20** zwanzig *tsvun-tsik*	**80** achtzig *akh-tsik*
3 drei *dry*	**9** neun *noyn*	**15** fünfzehn *fewnf-tsayn*	**30** dreißig *dry-sik*	**90** neunzig *noyn-tsik*
4 vier *feer*	**10** zehn *tsayn*	**16** sechzehn *zeks-tsayn*	**40** vierzig *feer-tsik*	**100** hundert *hoon-dairt*
5 fünf *fewnf*	**11** elf *elf*	**17** siebzehn *zeep-tsayn*	**50** fünfzig *fewnf-tsik*	**1,000** tausend *tow-zent*

ORDINAL NUMBERS

first erster *air-ster*	**fourth** vierter *feer-ter*	**seventh** siebter *zeep-ter*	**tenth** zehnter *tsayn-ter*
second zweiter *tsvy-ter*	**fifth** fünfter *fewnf-ter*	**eighth** achter *akh-ter*	**twentieth** zwanzigster *tsvun-stik-ster*
third dritter *drit-ter*	**sixth** sechster *zeks-ter*	**ninth** neunter *noyn-ter*	**hundredth** hundertster *hoon-dairt-ster*